In the Domain of
Mediumship

FRANCISCO CÂNDIDO XAVIER

In the Domain of Mediumship

BY THE SPIRIT ANDRE LUIZ

LIFE IN THE SPIRITUAL WORLD

INTERNATIONAL SPIRITIST COUNCIL

ISBN 85-98161-10-1

B.N. 369.206

Original Title:
NOS DOMÍNIOS DA MEDIUNIDADE

Translated by JUSSARA KORNGOLD
2ⁿᵈ **Edition** 2006 – published by the INTERNATIONAL SPIRITIST COUNCIL,
Brasília, (BR) – 2ⁿᵈ impression 3.000

5,01-AM; 000.1-O; 5/2006

Cover design by: ALESSANDRO FIGUEREDO

Layout: CLAUDIO CARVALHO

Copyright 2005 by
FEDERAÇÃO ESPÍRITA BRASILEIRA
Brasília (DF) – Brasil

Edition of
INTERNATIONAL SPIRITIST COUNCIL
Av. L-2 Norte – Q. 603 – Conjunto F (SGAN)
70830-030 – Brasília (DF) - Brazil

Authorized edition by Federação Espírita Brasileira

Printed and bound by
the Editorial and Graphics Department of Federação Espírita Brasileira
Rio de Janeiro (RJ) – Brazil
CNPJ nº 33.644.857/0002-84   *I.E. nº 81.600.503*

CIP-BRASIL. CATALOGAÇÃO-NA-FONTE
SINDICATO NACIONAL DOS EDITORES DE LIVROS, RJ.

L979i
2.ed.

Luiz, André (Spirit)
    In the domain of mediumship / by the Spirit André Luiz; [received
by Francisco Cândido Xavier]; translated by Jussara Korngold. – 2.
ed. – Brasília (Brasil): International Spiritist Council, 2006
    328p.: 21cm

    Translation of: Nos domínios da mediunidade
    ISBN 85-98161-10-1

    1. Spirit writings. 2. Spiritualism. I. Xavier, Francisco Cândido,
1910-2002. II. Conselho Espírita Internacional. III. Titie.

05-2693.   CDD 133.93
                                  CDU 133.7

24.08.05   29.08.05   011390

Table of Contents

Preface to the English Edition

Andre Luiz's collection of books, of which the present book is a part, is at the same time revealing, doctrinal and scientific. The 15 books of that collection in great part complete previous works about life after death by authors such as Swedenborg, A. Jackson Davis, Reverend G. Vale Owen and others. The books *"Nosso Lar – A Spiritual Home," "Disobsession," "The Messengers,"* and *"And Life Goes On"* are part of that collection.

Andre Luiz offers us in this book a valuable and remarkable account of his experiences when studying the subject of mediumship. *In the Domain of Mediumship* is pivotal for all those who seriously and responsibly desire to approach mediumship. At the same time that its reading is extremely enlightening it is also written in Andre Luiz's particularly captivating way, which envelops the reader's attention through the last page.

Those who are engaged in the work of translation know how challenging it can be for translators to depict the poetic nuances of the original author, not to mention the depth of his or her ideas. The richness of one language very seldom can be integrally expressed in a different one. However, the message of this precious book has to be sent to everyone, and we stretched our ability to the utmost in order to accomplish this endeavor.

Our main concern was to be completely faithful to the original transmission, but with an eye on preserving the beauty and smoothness of its content in the English language.

This book, and the many others that followed, were all dictated in Portuguese, and have guided hundreds of thousands of readers toward a more profound understanding of the reality that lies beyond death. They have been channeled by Francisco Cândido Xavier (1910 – 2002)

Francisco "Chico" de Paula Cândido Xavier was Brazil's most respected medium, a position of great moral authority in a country where an estimated 32 million people believe in Spiritism. Brazil has the world's largest spiritist population, and, in a career spanning of 75 years, Xavier became its most important figure.

Xavier was born into a poor family of nine brothers and sisters, in the suburbs of Belo Horizonte. Even though barely educated, he published 412 books – the Spirits of dead people dictated the texts to him through mediumship. His books sold an estimated 25 million copies, the profits of which were all channeled into charity work. As a former fingerprint expert with the Brazilian Ministry of Agriculture, Xavier lived on meager wages before drawing his state pension.

Several of his books were translated into English, Esperanto, French, Greek, Japanese, etc.

Countless hours were dedicated to this work. Repeatedly revisions and the collaboration of many supporting friends were required so that we could complete this translation.

We are particularly grateful to all those who have contributed toward this endeavor, Barbara Paulin, Danny Claudio, João Korngold, José Carlos da Silva Silveira, Crisley Thomé, Marcia Lacerda, Sandra Pizani, and Henrique de Sá, who inspired us to undertake the translation of this book.

Our heartfelt gratitude to Marie Levinson who worked tireless with me during the entire process of the translation of this book, scouring the manuscript for errors countless times, striving for perfection, with the sole desire of seeing this work accomplished. Finally, we would like to express our gratitude to Edward Christie, who contributed with his work and dedication during the final editing of this book.

We are grateful to the divine protection that accompanied us throughout this project.

Jussara Korngold
New York, 2005

Rays, Waves, Mediums, Minds

Studying the constitution of matter, science of the 20th century found many surprises that brought about radical revisions of long-held beliefs. Almost five centuries prior to Christ, Leucippus, the teacher of Democritus, theorized that every object was formed by infinitesimal particles (atoms) in constant motion. Despite this, classical culture continued to base itself in the four principles of Aristotelian thought (water, earth, air and fire) and in the three hypostatical elements of ancient alchemists (sulfur, salt and mercury) to explain the many combinations in the physical world.

In the 19th century, Dalton proposed the existence of atoms and that each element had their own individual weight. A marvelous period of intelligent investigations commenced, renewing the ideas and concepts of the so-called "indivisible particle." Extraordinary discoveries opened up new horizons to human knowledge:

Crooks discovers the radiant matter and studies the cathode rays.

Roentgen experiments with a Crookes tube shielded by heavy black cardboard and discovers X-Rays.

Henri Becquerel, seduced by this investigation, experiments with uranium looking for some radiation similar to that of this element, and finds out unexpected questions to be answered.

Mr. and Mrs. Curie, intrigued by this enigma, analyze tons of uranium and discover radium.

Old scientific theories lose their bases.

Rutherford, at the forefront of numerous pioneers, works out the nature of particles given off by radioactive materials.

The atom is discovered in the very forms in which it tries to hide, revealing solutions to what was once a mystery.

Since the last quarter of the 19th century, our concept of Earth has become that of a kingdom of waves and rays, currents and vibrations. Everything pulses with electricity and magnetism, movement and attraction. The study of cosmic rays proves the immense energies spread throughout the Universe, providing the physicists with a powerful opportunity for the investigation of atomic and sub-atomic phenomena.

Bohrs, Planck, Einstein elaborate new and great scientific theories.

The body is now understood to be no more than an electronic whirlwind guided by our conscience. Each tangible body is a bundle of concentrated energy. Matter is transformed into energy, which gives way to matter again.

As investigators of the truth, contemporary chemists and physicists, geometricians and mathematicians are, without intending it, priests of the Spirit. As a consequence of their constant studies, materialism and atheism will disappear for lack of a foundation in which to base their negative conclusions.

The laboratories are temples in which intelligence is dedicated to the service of God. Even when this intellectual activity is misguided, temporarily subordinated to the political hegemony that generates wars, the progress of science is divinely led, exalting goodness en route toward a glorious future. That future belongs to the Spirit!

Meditating on the future of Earth, Andre Luiz organized these knowledgeable pages regarding mediumship. He shows the importance of the spiritual interchange between human beings. The greater the advancement in their spiritual evolution, the more assuredly humans will understand it is wrong to think that death signals the end of a soul's existence. And now, more than ever, human beings see themselves as consciences embodied in provisionally united forces with the purpose of learning.

As the individual gradually understands that the tomb is an open door toward renovation, just as the cradle is the access toward experience, they grasp that their presence on the planet is a journey for their own progress, as well as that of the universe. In this great pilgrimage, we are all instruments of the forces with which we are in tune. Each person, with the sentiments that characterize their interior life, emits specific rays and lives in the spiritual wavelength with which they identify themselves. We are all mediums operating within the mental field that is appropriate to us: edifying if our thoughts flow in the direction of the superior life, or disturbing and depressing if we submit to the shadows of a primitive and tortured life.

Such truths shall not remain as matters of faith. Instead, they will emerge from the temples of science as mathematic equations. While various apprentices focus on their mediumship, studying it from Earth toward Heaven, our friend Andre Luiz tries to analyze and evaluate it from Heaven to Earth, thus collaborating in the construction of this new age.

What is most sublime in these pages is the necessity of keeping Christ in our hearts and conscience, so that we do not become disoriented upon coming in contact with the mediumistic phenomenon. Without the notion of responsibility, without devotion to the practice of goodness, without love of studying, without a persevering effort in our personal moral refinement, the liberating pilgrimage toward the peaks of life is impossible.

Andre Luiz' message is clear; therefore we do not have to interpret his meaning. Each medium has his or her own mind; each mind, with its unique rays that personalizes observations and interpretations. And, according to the rays that we emit, we shall establish our own spiritual environment in the wavelength of the thoughts with which our souls have attuned. In summary, this is equivalent to repeating with Jesus: "To each one according to one's deeds." (Mt. 16:27)

EMMANUEL

Pedro Leopoldo, October 3, 1954

1
Studying Mediumship

"Undoubtedly," agreed Aulus, "mediumship is one of the most intriguing fields in the world today. As humans approach the era of the Spirit, they will require cooperation of many so that they are ready for enlightenment."

The instructor Aulus, with his amiable and noble countenance, had admitted us into a brief course about mediumship at the request of Minister Clarencio.

Our mentor dedicated years of study to this specialized work, so in him we found the teacher we needed. As he spoke of the human needs, he fixed his firm and lucid attention on us, not unlike an older brother or tender father. Hilario and I could hardly contain our admiration. It was a privilege to hear him discuss the topic that brought us together and we were filled with admiration for him.

Allied within him was a rich cultural essence and the greatest capacity of love. He spoke of the course humanity had to take with the warmth of a benevolent and wise doctor, who would do the work of a nurse in order to assist in the cure of others.

Aulus had been interested in mediumistic experiments since 1779 when he met Mesmer, the well-known magnetizer, in Paris during the time the latter conducted research that would result in the renowned proposals he introduced. He also witnessed the accomplishments of Allan Kardec in codifying Spiritism. He was close to Cahagnet, Balzac, Théophile Gautier and Victor Hugo, ending his days in France after decades dedicated to mediumship and magnetism. In the spiritual world, he continued his observations, working towards his mission to educate. He has dedicated himself to the task of the spiritualization of Brazil for over thirty years.

Aulus provided us with the knowledge of his memories and experiences. He commented optimistically regarding a new field of action and he agreed to clarify his ideas for us. Marveling at him as we did, however, we had trouble responding to his questions.

"We are familiar with some aspects of spiritual interchange." I told Aulus. "Our desire, however, is to further our knowledge of this complex subject. Previously, we made cursory studies of *psychography,*[1] trance communication and materialization. In spite of this, our knowledge is still insignificant compared to the many facets of mediumship.

The mentor, kindly, assented to elucidating us. He cooperated in several departments and would give us which he humbly considered "simple notations."

To begin, Aulus invited us to listen to a friend speak about mediumship to a small group of students — incarnates and discarnates — and whose precise words he considered opportune and valuable. We immediately accepted and, having no time to waste, we quickly followed him.

In the vast section of the Ministry of Communications we were introduced to the instructor, Alberio, who was about to commence his dissertation. We sat down among dozens of companions, in attentive and silent expectation. As with many other mentors that I knew, Alberio went up to the lectern unceremoniously, as if he were simply a brother who was going to converse with us fraternally.

"My friends," he said with assurance, "as we continue our studies, let us consider that the mind is the basis of all mediumistic phenomena.

---

[1]**N.T.:** Psychography: Involuntary or unconscious writing, as by a medium." Funk and Wagnalls, New Comprehensive International Dictionary of the English Language, Encyclopedia Edition.

"We recognize that the universe, which extends itself into the infinite with millions of suns, is the externalization of divine thought whose essence we receive as eternal wisdom, inasmuch as our spiritual evolvement allows. From the superstructure of the heavenly bodies to the sub-atomic infrastructure, everything is contained in the mind of God, just as fish and aquatic plants are contained in the immense ocean.

"We are children of the Creator and from Him we inherit the faculty of creating, developing, nurturing and transforming. The conceptual dimensions in which we find ourselves circumscribe our lives, and we recognize our insignificance compared to the glory of the Spirits that have already reached an angelic state. Yet we all radiate the active energy of our own thoughts, establishing the psychic ambient correlating to our individuality.

"Each world possesses a field of electromagnetic tension within a gravitational force that maintains its equilibrium. Similarly, each soul finds its place with life forces that have affinity with its mental halo; that is to say in the sphere of the individuals it needs to make adjustments or for spiritual advancement.

"Each planet makes its revolutions in the orbit to which it is assigned by the laws of equilibrium without exceeding them, just as each conscience evolves within the spiritual group that influences its actions. We are a vast group of intelligences, synchronized in one vibratory grade of perception, integrating billions of souls that are humankind on Earth. Each world harbors a family of the universal humanity and we are but one of these families.

"Up to now, we perceived only the expressions of the life that touches us, limited by our understanding. Depending on our brothers in our trajectory toward evolvement, like the worlds that move in space influenced by the stars surrounding them, we act and react upon each other through the mental energy with which we become renovated. We are constantly creating, feeding and destroying forms and situations, landscapes and things in the structuring of our own destinies.

"Our mind is, in this manner, a nucleus of intelligent forces generating a subtle plasma that, upon exteriorizing incessantly away from us, offers objective resources to the images of our own imagination under the command of our personal designs. The idea is an entity organized by our spirit, to which our thoughts give form or shape and our will imprints movement and direction. From the conjunction of our ideas our own personal existence results."

The orator made a small pause that no one dared to interrupt, and later proceeded:

"All living beings breathe in the psychic wavelength that is unique to them, within the dimensions that are characteristic to them, or in the frequency that is particular to them. That psyche does not depend on the

21

central nervous system once it is flowing from the mind. It is, then, the one that conditions all the phenomenon of organic life within itself."

"Upon examining animic values as a faculty of communication between the Spirits, in whichever sphere they find themselves, we cannot lose sight of the mental world of the agent and of the receiver. The receiver's intelligence is colored by the thoughts in which it lives. The sender's intelligence submits to the limits and to the interpretations of the thoughts that it is capable of producing.

"Backward discarnate[2] natives, communicating with wise individuals, who are still attached to the physical body, can only offer to them trivial subjects concerning their primitive experiences on Earth. Conversely, wise people without their physical body, entering into a relationship with backward natives attached to their African habitat, will not succeed in giving them their immediate cooperation, unless they could assist them with their mental interests, as in helping a herd of bovine or in curing an illness of the material body. For this reason, a backward native

---

[2] **N.T.:** Discarnate: According to *Webster*'s 10th Edition, is an obsolete word meaning "having no physical body." In the Spiritist philosophy it is widely used as both a noun and an adjective to describe a nonphysical but conscious individuality. The *American Heritage Dictionary of the English Language*: Fourth Edition – 2000 PAdjective: Having no material body or form: a discarnate spirit. Etymology: dis + (in)carnate. Other forms: **dis·carnate** – NOUN.
The word discarnate is used in this book in its noun and adjective sense.

would not feel happy in the company of a wise person; likewise, a wise person would not be detained by a backward native for lack of that nourishment, almost imponderable, which we could classify as *vibrational compensations.*

"It is a law that our greatest happiness is received from those with whom we can exchange mental values similar to our own. This is comparable to a tree that produces better when situated among the same species with which it can germinate.

"In mediumship, we cannot overlook the phenomenon of synchronization. We attract Spirits that have affinity with us and to which we are also attracted. If it is true that each person gives according to what he or she has, then it is unquestionable that each one receives according to what he or she gives.

"The mind is the basis of all mediumistic manifestations in whatever manner they are expressed. Therefore, it is indispensable that we use moral and cultural treasures to expand our thinking. The values expressed in them make it possible to fixate the light that descends toward us from the highest realms, through the genius of wisdom and love that oversees our experiences.

"Those that compared our mental world to a mirror were right: we reflect the images around us, and we direct toward others the images that we create. And, since we cannot escape the imperative of attraction, we shall only present clarity and beauty if they exist in the mirror of our interior life.

"Mental reflections either favor our procrastination or compel us to go forward. Each person lives in the heaven or hell that one builds for oneself in the innermost recesses of one's heart and mind, independently of the physical body. Observing life in its glorious eternity, death is solely a transition between two types of a similar experience, in the *indestructible today.*

"We encounter mediumship wherever human beings develop. Sanctifying missions and battles of destruction, noble tasks and evil obsessions, all have their origin in the reflections of the individual or in the collective mind, combined with the sublime or degrading forces of the thoughts that nurture them. Therefore, let us learn to cultivate our desire for education and perfect ourselves each day. We are all mediums, no matter what we do.

"Psychic strength is natural to all individuals, but mediumistic perfection without the refinement or purification of the individual is not possible. It is counterproductive to intensify the movement of energy without disciplining our impulses and it is dangerous to possess this ability without knowledge of its proper use.

"The mirror buried in the mud does not reflect the splendor of the Sun. An agitated lake does not reflect the image of the star that exists in the infinite.

Let us elevate our level of knowledge with appropriate study and let us purify our emotions through the constant exercise of superior virtues. We need to do this if we wish to receive the message of the great souls.

"Mediumship in itself is not enough. It is essential to know what type of mental wavelength we are assimilating to, so that we can recognize the quality of our work and evaluate the direction taken."

Alberio continued to make valuable comments and later responded to complicated questions asked by several apprentices. As for my part, I received plenty on which to meditate. With a few words of appreciation, Hilario and I said goodbye to our instructors. Aulus promised to meet with us on the following day.

2

The Psychoscope

When we returned the following night, Aulus again graciously received us.

"I believe I have charted our program," he told us paternally. He paused, observed us attentively, and continued.

"We should keep studying a small group where our observations may be of the highest quality. We have a group of ten incarnate companions; four of whom are mediums with a respectable moral base and who regularly practice their faculty. This small group is in the service of an institution dedicated to our Christian ideal. From that group, we can extract notes and gather information valuable to us."

He observed us kindly in silence for an instant, and added:

That is why you desire specialized knowledge of mediumship in the terrestrial sphere. Were we to confine our study to our circle of spiritual activity, the subject would be less complex."

"Yes" – Hilario and I agreed. "We want to be of some assistance to those incarnate brothers who are dedicated and committed to serving. For that reason, this opportunity comes to us as a veritable blessing."

We warmly exchanged ideas for a few minutes. Aulus then extended his sincere invitation.

"Let us proceed. There is no time to lose."

He picked up a small box and noticing our curiosity, he said calmly:

"We have here a *psychoscope* which will facilitate our examinations and studies without having to tax our mental concentration."

He asked me to take it with us. I picked up the enigmatic instrument that on Earth would not weigh more than a few grams. I was curious, but it was Hilario who asked without delay:

"Psychoscope? What kind of new invention is that?"

"It is an apparatus to which an illustrious student of spiritual phenomenology intuitively made reference at the end of the last century. It is designed to observe the soul and define its vibrations at the same time that it studies physical matter," Aulus explained with a smile. "We expect that in the future this will also be available to human beings. It functions with electricity and magnetism, utilizing radiant elements analogous to gamma rays. It has a magnifying lens that can also be used for microphotography."

While we proceeded in the direction of the terrestrial city in which we were to work, the mentor continued:

"In our supervisory task, we are able to classify without difficulty the probabilities of the different groups of psychic services that exist in the world. By analyzing the psychoscopy of a person or a group of workers, it is possible to deduce their potential and qualify the category of their status. According to the radiation they project, we can plan the work they are capable of achieving."

My colleague and I could not hide our surprise. Surprised and shocked, Hilario asked:

"Can anyone of us be submitted to an exam of this nature?"

"Without a doubt," answered the interlocutor good-naturedly. "We are all subject to examination by the superior planes in the same manner that we currently investigate the planes below ours. If the spectroscope permits the individual to investigate the nature of the chemical elements found at enormous distances by analyzing the luminous waves that they emit, with greater facility we will identify the values of a human by the rays one emits. We can know of one's morals, sentiments, education and character through a brief observation."

"But," questioned Hilario, "based on the hypothesis that evil elements emerge in an otherwise good group, would the Spiritual Instructors expel them as a result of what an analysis from the psychoscope revealed?"

"It would not be necessary. If the majority is dedicated to the practice of goodness, the minority, who are prisoners of evil, will eventually withdraw from the group owing to lack of affinity."

"Notwithstanding," added my companion, "what would happen in an institution whose elevated program has degenerated into disharmony, where virtue there is nothing more than a fiction that hides ignorance and perversity?"

"In this case," responded the mentor serenely, "we would not resort to any form of intervention or accusation, as life itself is in charge of situating each individual in the place which belongs to oneself."

Smiling, he added: "The angels or ministers of eternal wisdom entrust us with the renovating forces of time and experience. A gram of radium loses ½ gram of its weight in sixteen centuries. A cyclotron working with atomic projectiles accelerated to millions of electrons-volts immediately achieves the transmutation of the chemical elements. We are also perfected either through slow evolution throughout the millenniums, or with an abrupt strike of suffering that alters our mental panorama."

We reflected over his words. Our mentor had both a brilliant intellectual background and a faculty for explanation. I was planning to ask questions not directly related to the program but before I had the chance, Aulus spoke.

"All noble conversation is instructive; however, for now, let us proceed with our preoccupation and stay fixed on the task. To achieve success in our task we must pay close attention to it. If we were to digress into chemistry, it would only delay us."

Focusing once again on our objectives, Hilario repeated: "The psychoscope gives us a motive for important considerations. Try to imagine a human society that could take a picture of the interior life of its members. That would save much time in solving numerous psychological problems."

"Yes," added the mentor cordially, "the future holds miracles for the reasoning of the common individual."

We had now reached the gate to the spacious building that the mentor said was the sanctuary where we were to visit and serve.

"This is a Christian Spiritist Center. The work that goes on here will provide us an opportunity for experience and observation." Upon entering a spacious enclosure where there were numerous unfortunate discarnate entities, the mentor advised:

"Here we have the room dedicated to public teaching. However, the nucleus that we are seeking is situated in a private area, somewhat like the location of the heart within the body."

After a few moments, we cautiously entered the room in which a small group was gathered in silent concentration.

"Our companions", explained the mentor, "are engaged in preparatory harmonization. They dedicate fifteen minutes to prayer, or use this time for explanation or reading on moral subjects. They are aware that they need a noble and dignified attitude to participate in spiritual tasks, since this makes it possible to attract evolved companions. Therefore, they do not appear here without bringing the best that they possess."

Hilario and I were inclined to inquire further; however, the respectable vibrations present in the room demanded silence. Friends from our sphere remained in quiet prayer, obliging us to silently concentrate as well. The mentor put the psychoscope in place and, after adjusting it, invited us to look through it.

When it was my turn, the peculiarities of the equipment amazed me. With little effort, I noticed that all physical matter assumed a different appearance, emphasizing the matter of the spirit world. The roof, the walls and other objects appeared made of currents of energy that emitted an opaque clarity.

I stopped to contemplate the incarnate companions, who were united by vast radiant circles that hovered over their heads in an opal-like splendor. Looking at the opaque block of semi-dark mass to which the table was reduced, I noticed a crown of solar light formed of ten characteristic points, springing forth from the center of each one the spiritual face of our incarnate friends in prayer.

A wide violet light extended from that chain of golden lights. It appeared to be contained in another strip of orange light in diverse tones, which at that moment I could not distinguish. My attention was fixed on the circle of the shiny faces strongly united one to the other, somewhat like ten small suns chained to one another. I noticed that above each was a halo of almost vertical rays, brilliant and moving, as if they were small antennae of smoked gold. Over these crowns, which were distinguishable from one companion to the other, an abundant cluster of luminous stars fell from on High, touching the heads that were joined. They appeared as soft currents of energy that transformed into microscopic petals. These petals ignited and darkened in a myriad of delicate and capricious forms, gravitating momentarily around the brains that were producing them, creating the impression of satellites of brief existence swirling around the vital spring from which they emanated.

Spiritual Mentors, as custodians of the assembly, were watching over, each one radiating his own light. Amazed by the brothers from the physical plane who were thus revealing an affinity with the brilliant wavelength that enveloped them, I asked enthusiastically:

"Dear friend Aulus, are the companions that we are visiting, by any chance, high initiates in the Divine Revelation?"

The mentor made a good-humored gesture as he responded:

"No, we are still very far from such apostles. We are here in the company of four sisters and six brothers of goodwill. They are common people. They eat, drink, dress and present themselves on Earth similar to everyone else. However, they have their minds set on active faith and service, expressed through their love for their fellow beings. They make every effort to discipline themselves, exercise renouncement and cultivate charity. Through their personal efforts in righteousness and study they have acquired an elevated level of mental radiation.

Hilario, who had utilized the psychoscope first, added in the admiring tone of a surprised child:

"But what about the light? It transfigured matter with a clarity that was magnificent!"

"Nothing is strange!" – replied the mentor affectionately. "Don't you know registered in the heart of the individual is an electromagnetic force of one oscillation per second? Do you, by chance, ignore that all living substances on Earth emit energies focused in the gamma of ultraviolet radiations? Our companions are souls who are regularly evolved and who have appreciably good vibratory conditions because of their sincere devotion to righteousness, and by their disregard of personal desires. They can, in this way, project mental rays of sublimation, thus assimilating higher currents and enriching the vital mental rays they generate, similar to common dynamos."

"Vital rays? – asked my colleague, seeking clarification.

"Yes. In order to give you a clearer definition, let's call them rays of ectoplasm, to use the technical vocabulary of the modern spiritists. These rays are found in all living beings. It is through them that the caterpillars realize their complex metamorphosis, and it is also due to them that mediumistic materialization occurs. It is through sensitive incarnates that these helpful, liberating energies are processed more easily All beings, however, emit them in a frequency that varies according to the tasks that life has assigned to them."

And with optimism, he added:

"Mediumship is affirmed on the basis of the mind, with its prodigious field of radiations. The knowledge of rays will imprint, in a brief time, a great renovation in the diverse cultural sectors of the world. But we must wait for the future."

Immediately thereafter, Aulus invited us to participate in a more direct inspection, one for which we gladly accompanied him.

3

Mediumistic Team

"Let us get acquainted with our mediumistic team," said Aulus.

Stopping near an incarnate companion in charge of directing the tasks, he said:

"This is our brother Raul Silva, the director of this group, who is totally devoted to fraternity. Accurate in his duties and of ardent faith, he brings to the group a deep comprehension and goodwill. Because of the love with which he conducts his task, he is a faithful instrument of discarnate benefactors, who find in his mind a crystal mirror that reproduces their instructions without distortion."

He then directed his attention to a young lady and, pointing her out, explained:

"This is our sister Eugenia, a docile medium who promises to have a brilliant future in the expansion of goodness. She is an excellent instrument of transmission that assists disoriented discarnate Spirits. With a clear intuition allied to her moral base, she has the advantage of remaining conscious during the communications and so benefits our field of action."

He stopped on the left side of a young man who appeared about 30 years old, and said:

"Here we have our friend Anelio Araujo. He has been gradually progressing in clairvoyance, clairaudience and psychography."

Then, approaching a nice companion, he notified us:

"This is our collaborator Antonio Castro, a well-intentioned young man who has a promising future in our activities. Being an unconscious medium, he still requires great vigilance on our part. He departs from his physical body with ease and achieves valuable tasks, but he requires greater study and wider experiences to express more clearly his personal observations. At times, he behaves as a child when separated from his body, compromising our activities. When he lends his body to demented or suffering entities, he requires our assistance, as he usually yields his body to the will of the communicating Spirit. As you know, it is his obligation to assist us in containing them, so that our fraternal efforts do not result in injury to his physical body. He is, nonetheless, a valuable assistant in our studies."

Moving along a little more, the mentor stopped in front of a respectable lady who had been in ardent prayer, and exclaimed:

"I would like to introduce our sister Celina, a devoted companion of our spiritual ministry. She is 50 years old and has made significant victories in her moral battles. She has been a widow for almost twenty years, dedicated to her children with admirable valor, overcoming thorny obstacles and dark days of renunciation. She was able to heroically withstand the assault from ignorant and unfortunate legions of Spirits that surrounded her husband, whom she married in order to fulfill a sacrificial task. She witnessed the persecution of evil geniuses to which she did not surrender. In fulfilling her obligations, her conduct has been irreproachable.

"She refined her mediumship, perfecting it with the flames of moral suffering, as you would mold heated iron with raps on an anvil. She is not a simple instrument of psychic phenomena, but a dedicated worker in constructing spiritual values. She is a clairvoyant, a clairaudient, and an unconscious trance medium, as well as a medium of out of body experiences. She enters these states with the same spontaneity with which she breathes, while staying true to her responsibilities. This makes her a valuable collaborator. She is diligent and humble, finding her greatest happiness in fraternal love. Distributing her time between obligations and edifying studies, she is like a battery assimilating beneficial spiritual energies. Because of that, she is less vulnerable to the forces of darkness."

It was true that standing next to her we enjoyed a sensation of peace and comfort. Most likely because of the current of indefinable happiness that inundated us, Hilario asked:

"If we were to make a psychoscopic analysis of Celina, would the conditions we are visualizing about her now be faithfully registered?"

"Perfectly," responded Aulus immediately. "Such an observation would ratify her emanations of kindness and understanding, faith and good humor. Just as scientific studies on Earth catalogue the chemical elements that form dense matter, in our field of rarefied matter it is possible to analyze the type of subtle forces that are emitted by each being.

"In the future, human beings will be able to examine emissions of optimism and confidence, sadness and desperation, and fix their density and limits just as they can now separate and study uranium atoms. These mental principles are immeasurable and worthy of special attention in the future of humankind, as with photons currently studied by the scientists engaged in deciphering the constitution of light."

After a brief interval the mentor added:

"A psychoscopic analysis determines the nature of our thoughts, and through this it is very simple to recognize our merits as well as our weaknesses."

The mentor invited us to participate in a detailed examination of the encephalic field of sister Celina, pointing out:

"In no mediumistic process can we forget that it is through the brain that the mind manifests. Surely, you already possess advanced knowledge regarding the corporeal body, so we don't need to discuss technical details about it. "

Caressing her hair, which showed strands of gray, he added:

"A succinct exam of the inter-cranial life will be sufficient, as it is there that we find the keys of communication between the mental and the physical world."

Centering our attention on a small lens that Aulus gave us, our friends' brain appeared similar to a powerful radio station with thousands of microscopic antennae and conductors, resistors and connections. They were used by specialized brain cells, functioning as detectors and stimulants, transformers and amplifiers of sensations and ideas whose vibrations shone within as incessant rays, illuminating a miniscule sky.

The mentor observed with us the marvelous labyrinth in which the epiphysis or pineal gland was shining like a tiny blue sun, and said:

"We are not going to point out minor things related to the brain or the nervous system in general, as you are already familiar with these through your knowledge of human nature."

At that instant I was amazed by a beam of light formed by the cortical cells vibrating with the magnetic flow of thoughts.

"Let us remember," continued the mentor, "that the delicate encephalic apparatus unites millions of cells, which function as if they were workers in a hierarchical order within the harmonious governmental structure."

And enumerating distinct regions of this prodigious thinking kingdom, he declared:

"There is no need to digress. The experiences acquired through the soul constitute a marvelous synthesis of perception and sensitivity in our condition of free Spirits. These experiences, however, are located in the corporeal body as controllers of the manifestations of individuality, and are perfectly analyzable. That is how the incarnate soul possesses, in the physical brain, the special centers that govern the head, the face, the eyes, the ears and limbs.

"The brain also governs the centers of speech, language, sight, audition, memory, writing, taste, swallowing, tact, smell, of registering hot and cold, pain, and muscular equilibrium. It is also controls the inner values of the mind, the connection with the exterior world, imagination, esthetic and artistic taste and many others treasured by the experiences of the soul, which conquers its own individuality, little by little, effort upon effort. This work in favor of its sublimity is possible through the avenues of progress and perfection that Earth offer."

A brief pause occurred spontaneously and, because Hilario and I did not want to interrupt, the mentor continued:

"We cannot study mediumistic faculties without a correlative study of the personality. Therefore, it is of great importance that we consider the cerebral centers, where thought and will operate. The cerebral centers influence all mediumistic phenomena, from pure intuition to objective materialization. Through their work of love and sacrifice, wise and benevolent Spirits use these centers as do humans when, as mediums, they maintain superior ideals of kindness and service. They are also available, however, to inferior and animalized entities through the lamentable process of obsession"

"But," interrupted Hilario wisely, "is it possible that less evolved intelligences could invade an illuminated cerebral field such as that of our sister Celina?"

"We cannot forget," said the mentor, "that Celina is an incarnate soul on a long trial, and as an apprentice, she is far from mastering all her lessons."

He meditated for a moment, and then philosophized good-humouredly:

"On a hundred mile trip, many surprises can occur in the last mile."

Then placing his paternal right hand over the forehead of the medium, he continued:

"Our sister is a testimony to goodwill, outstanding faith, charity and patience. Like all of us, she is not yet able to free herself from her past debts. We are a vast legion of fighters seeking to overcome the enemy that inhabits our interior nature or our very world, enemies symbolized by our past habits of living with an inferior nature. Such habits place us in tune with the inhabitants of the shadows, and in evident harm to our equilibrium.

"Our friend Celina, as well as all of us, must take care not to abandon our obligation that keeps us receptive to the light. To do so would be to yield to vanity and disenchantment, misleading us to consider them as acquired rights and unjustifiable misfortunes. If this occurs to her, it would certainly interrupt her noble ascension. Many mediums suffer losses of this type. After a promising and brilliant beginning, they claim possession of spiritual resources that do not belong to them, or they fear the prolonged afflictions along their pathways, and so become sterile and useless.

This can lower their moral level and, yielding to inertia, they may cultivate primitive impulses. Incessant work in righteousness would make them forget such inferior impulses."

Then, smiling, he added:

"We have not yet conquered the supreme victory over ourselves. The soil does not produce without the help of the plough or the hoe. Without working and struggling to perfect our potential, we would be permanently threatened by hazardous weeds, which would multiply easier when the best quality soil is abandoned.

Then, looking straight at us as if to emphasize the weight of the responsibilities with which we were vested, he concluded:

"Our present spiritual achievements are similar to small glimmering lights over the shadows of our past. We need great caution when planting the seeds of righteousness, so that the winds of evil do not sweep them away. That is why the mediumistic task, considered a tool for superior intelligences, is not easily attained. Through the fragile channel which lends itself to the passage of the light, we are attacked by the heavy waves of darkness and ignorance that become agitated and dense around us."

The mentor became quiet. He, too, was now connected to the magnetic field of the friends who followed silently, ready to commence the meeting.

4

In Service

A gentle knock on the door caused one of the companions, who had been meditating, to answer. A young lady and an older gentleman, accompanied by two family members, came inside and sat in a corner of the living room outside of the magnetic field.

"They are the patients who will receive assistance," informed the mentor.

Later, a Spirit collaborator invited to come in numerous ill and disturbed Spirits that were seated facing the assembly, creating a nurtured group. Not one of them came near us under constraint. Instead, they gathered around our incarnate friends encircled in prayer, like moths instinctively drawn to a great light.

They arrived excited, expressing incomplete phrases and making small talk. After receiving the emissions of the spiritual group, however, the disturbed Spirits became mute as though dominated by forces that they could not perceive. Attentively, Aulus told us:

"They are mentally tormented souls that accompany their relatives, friends or enemies to this institute's public reunions. They disassociate from the group as soon as the incarnates are renewed by the ideas of salvation, expressed by those who spread the doctrinal teachings. When the incarnates' thoughts are redirected, these Spirits become disoriented and feel sudden and radical changes in their minds."

"Some rebel and escape from the temples of prayer such as this one, temporarily hating our assistance and scheming to search out and persecute their victims. Others, touched by the lessons, remain where they received them, anxiously waiting for further clarification."

Hilario received this information with surprise, and asked curiously:

"What happens when the incarnates do not follow the lessons that they have been given?"

"They simply walk through the sanctuaries of faith like sealed vessels, impervious to good suggestions. They continue to be impenetrable to the need for change."

"Are these same phenomena repeated in other religious groups?"

"Yes. The spoken word plays a significant role in the construction of the spirit. Sermons and conferences from priests and speakers of different faiths, as long as they are inspired by infinite good, also aim for moral elevation."

The mentor meditated for an instant, and added:

"Among human beings, however, if it is not easy to cultivate a dignified life, it is even harder to prepare for a liberating death. As a rule, the soul dies without clearing out its confused thoughts of situations, persons and earthly matters. The mind, as a result, continues to be a prisoner of inferior worldly interests and faces disquieting scenes of its own imagination.

"The value of the respected religious community is that it contributes to the creation of an ambient for spiritual ascension. This has indispensable advantages, not solely for the incarnate Spirits who participate in it with sincerity and fervor, but also for the discarnates that aspire for their own transformation. Needy souls, who come without their dense bodies, fill the sanctuaries during their public activities, thirsting for relief. The speakers, preachers of the good word provoke the disassociation of mental attitudes by way of the liberating principles spread in the sphere of thought." He smiled in good humor, and continued:

"For this reason, entities that feed off others operate against the speakers, quite often surrounding listeners with disturbing energies that make them sleepy, delaying their renovation and progress."

Upon observing the troubled brothers that approached the people sitting in a semi-circle, I had a desire to use the psychoscope in order to examine them more closely. Aulus read my thoughts:

"It is not necessary. A careful analysis will suffice to provide us with interesting results, since our friends carry engraved in their very own perispiritual body[3] the sufferings that they experience."

I noticed that the mentor did not want a long conversation, most probably because he was preparing to collaborate in the tasks ahead. Therefore, I took advantage of those brief moments to observe the unfortunate companions who were linked up in a state of both anguish and expectancy.

They appeared to be covered by a great oval cloud, dark gray in color, thick and mobile, agitated by strange formations. I noticed that some were afflicted with mutilations, lesions, paralysis, and diverse forms of ulcerations as if they were still in physical life.

Perhaps because Hilario and I had an attitude of apprentices in school, one of the spiritual collaborators of the meeting approached us and cordially said:

"These suffering brothers and sisters bring along with them the stigma of errors they have deliberately

---

[3]**N.T.:** Also known as astral body – it is the body, wh--ich functions in the Astral or Spiritual World. It is composed of matter, relatively, however, much finer than that which composes the ordinary physical body. (Lewis Spence, *"The Encyclopedia of the Occult,"* page 41).

committed. Illnesses, as a result of moral unbalance, survive in the perispirit and are fed by the same thoughts that caused them, when these thoughts continue after the death of the corporeal body."

"But do they improve at the mediumship meeting?" inquired Hilario, timidly.

"Yes," responded the mentor. "They assimilate new ideas that gradually improve their inner vision and pave new destinies. Mental renovation is the renovation of life."

I meditated over the illusion of those who imagine that in death the soul is destined for those places of happiness or sorrow called, respectively, heaven and hell.

Few humans admit the evidence provided by our thoughts, activities and accomplishments: that, in death, we will see all that we hide under our corporeal dress. Conscience is a force of self-generated goodness and evil.

We faced a long row of suffering souls in the purgatories they themselves created. We were nearing a companion with a withered and sad expression, to whom Hilario compassionately asked:

"Friend, what is your name?"

"Me?" – replied the one questioned. He tried hard to remember, and then answered: "I do not have a name."

"Impossible," answered my colleague incredulously. "We all have names."

"I forgot...I forgot everything," responded the disconsolate one.

"This is a case of amnesia to be studied," explained the spiritual companion of the work team we were visiting.

"Is this a natural phenomenon?" asked Hilario, doubtfully.

"Yes, it can be due to an imbalance brought from Earth, as it is possible that our friend is a victim of vigorous post-hypnotic suggestion. The suggestion may have originated with a persecutor exercising a strong control over the victim's memory. Our friend still finds himself profoundly attached to physical sensations, and these mold his cerebral life. Considering this, it is probable that he is controlled by a strange and dishonest will to which he may have been acquainted."

"Heavens!" – exclaimed my colleague, quite impressed. "Is such control possible after death?"

"Yes, of course. Death is a continuation of life, and in our eternal life we possess what we seek."

Remembering that we were studying mediumship, I observed:

"If our forgetful friend were taken to a medium, would he communicate like this and ignore his identity?"

"Precisely, and he would require warm loving attention as in any common mental case. Speaking through any medium that gives him access, he would be for any counselor on Earth the same enigma that we are now witnessing."

At that moment, a Spirit in a deplorable state approached us. He was a thin and sad man, whose right arm was paralyzed and dry. Responding to my questioning glance, Aulus, appearing to have little time to spare in conversation, just said:

"Observe him. Examine him yourself."

I approached him touching his forehead gently, and I could sense his anguish. In the crystallized memories of his mental world, his intimate drama was revealed. He had been a muscle bound stevedore on the docks and a drunkard. One day returning home, his father disapproved his conduct, provoking his son to beat him. Unable to return the attack the old man, spitting blood, yelled menacingly:

"Infamous one, your cruel arm shall be transformed into a dry branch."

Upon listening to these words, spoken with intense hypnotic force, the son returned to the public highway. Stunned by the evil wish, he continued to drink in order to forget. Drunk and unable to maintain his equilibrium, he was in a street-car accident and lost his arm.

He lived for a few years more, but he clung to the memory of his father's vengeful oath that was engraved deep in his heart. For this reason, after death, the mutilated arm was restored to him hanging dry and inert in the perispiritual body.

While reflecting, our mentor again came nearer to us and perceiving what was happening, he informed us:

"It is a very difficult case of readjustment that requires time and tolerance."

Placing his hands on the shoulders of the invalid, he added:

"Our friend's mind is subjugated by the remorse that has affected him since the day that he received the curse. To restore himself, he requires great affection."

Without forgetting the subject that held our attention, I inquired:

"If this companion were to communicate through a medium, would his sensations be perceived by the human receptor?"

"Yes, of course," agreed the mentor. "He would reflect in the passive medium the impressions that control him, through the magnetic processes in which the services of interchange are based."

He smiled, kindly, and added:

"Meanwhile, let us not get lost in particular cases. Each entity of the many unbalanced ones that are united here brings disquieting experiences. Let's observe this from a better vantage."

He then conducted me to the head of the table where our friend, Raul Silva was ready to commence the prayer.

5

Assimilating Mental Energies

The time was 7:58 pm when the spiritual director made his entrance into the small enclosure. Our guide introduced everyone. Brother Clementino greeted us warmly.

"The house belongs to all," he said with a smile. "Therefore, be content and ready for the task for which we have prepared."

At that moment, diverse entities from the Spirit world moved closer to the mediums, which were ready to commence the service   Clementino moved toward Raul Silva and remained in silent reflection.

Aulus invited me to use the psychoscope and adjusting it in a different manner, he recommended I observe carefully. The incarnate companions were immersed in mental concentration and they looked different compared to our previous examination. The physical bodies appeared to conduct electromagnetic waves of elevated intensity. The nervous system, the glandular nucleuses and the plexus emitted a particular kind of luminescence. The mind, placing itself in close proximity with the brain, appeared as a sphere of light and each companion had his own radiation potential.

Calling our attention to this curious point, the guide explained: "In any mediumistic study we should not forget that spiritual individuality resides in the physical body formed from the world's resources. Blood, brain, nerves, bones, skin and muscles unite for the manifestation of the soul on Earth. These elements constitute the temporary clothes needed to suit the environment in which the soul finds itself."

Brother Clementino placed his hand over the forehead of the friend who was directing the meeting. At that moment, he appeared to be more human than Spirit.

"The spiritual benefactor who is now directing us," said the instructor, "appears denser and darker because he lowered his normally elevated vibration to match Raul's in order to begin the task at hand. He now acts upon Raul's cerebral life, somewhat like an emeritus musician would respectfully handle a valuable violin of whose quality he is aware."

Flashes of light started to emit from Clementino's head. At the same time, Silva's brain, under the influence of the benefactor's hand, was alive with an intense but diverse illumination. The discarnate mentor raised his voice to implore divine blessings, moving us with familiar expressions, which Raul transmitted in a loud voice with near perfect fidelity.

Our emotions aroused, a profound and passive silence reigned. Threads of brilliant lights circled around all the participants of the table; we could see that the prayer had brought all of them together more completely.

After the prayer, I approached Raul. I wanted to investigate first hand the sensations that controlled his physical sphere. I observed that his physique, including his arms and legs, were under a vigorous current of energy that made his skin bristle, producing an excitingly sweet sensation similar to a refreshing shiver. This current rested over his solar plexus where it transformed into a luminous stimulus that spread through the nervous system to the brain. This stimulus flowed from his mouth in the form of words. Following my analysis, the mentor explained:

"Brother Clementino's mental forces affected the psyche of Raul, as electricity acts upon an electric bulb. Pressing upon the solar plexus, it rises toward the neuro-cerebral system, much like electricity from a transmitting station reaches a bulb, expanding through the incandescent filaments to produce light."

"And what about the voltage problem?" I inquired with curiosity.

"It is not overlooked. Clementino graduates his thoughts and expressions according to Raul's capacity as well as the surrounding ambient. In a similar way, the electrical technician controls the projection of energy according to the network's receptive elements."

Good-humoredly, he added:

"Each recipient receives according to his receptive capacity."

The comparisons Aulus made suggested interesting questions. Electrical energy generates the light in a bulb. But how are the energy and the bulb related? The spiritual contact triggered the forces that emanated from Raul's brain and mouth in the form of luminous rays and words. The instructor perceived our thoughts and quickly explained:

"The bulb, in whose interior the light is produced, disperses the photons which are elements of nature that vibrate in physical movements particular to them. Our soul, in whose intimate ambient the radiating idea is processed, projects the condensed spiritual elements into various mental forces. The worlds act one upon the other through the radiation they expel, and the souls are influenced via the mental agents that they produce."

The precise and serene words of the mentor led us into a short meditation. The clear references regarding the mental energy brought beautiful reflections. It occurred to me that thought is limited by the reality of the corporeal world.

Just as we on Earth have an understanding of the chemistry of dense matter, we can also study the make-up of the mind. Cruel thoughts, rebellion, sadness, love, comprehension, hope and happiness have individual weights and make the soul more dense or subtle. In addition, we can define its magnetic qualities. Each mental wavelength possesses its characteristic force expressed in silent concentration, speech or written word.

We are victims or beneficiaries of our own thoughts according to the mental energies that we project. Thus, we enslave ourselves by our own erroneous thoughts or liberate ourselves toward progress, according to how what we determine and accomplish harmonizes with eternal laws.

Our mentor, attentive to the objectives of our presence in the Center, interrupted this soliloquy and asked: "Have you noticed the fellowship between Clementino and Silva during the moment of prayer?"

Wanting to hear his answer, he continued:

"Here we witness a perfect assimilation of thoughts that usually precedes mediumistic activity. To clarify, let us compare Raul's physical body to a broadcasting station receptor. The mental emissions of Clementino, condensing his thoughts and will, envelope Raul in rays that reach his interior sphere. This is achieved primarily through the pores of the skin, functioning as a myriad of antennae, and through which the emission acquires weak and indecisive impressions. Those impressions are supported by the spiritual body's centers of force that act as condensers and immediately reach the nervous system. They instantly wind into coils that reconstitute themselves in the brain, where hundreds of motor centers similar to electromagnets are connected to each other.

"In this dynamic nucleus, the mental actions of thought are processed by the brain as a powerful broadcasting station and of words by the mouth as an effective speaker. Such stimulus is also expressed through the mechanisms of the hands, feet, senses and organs, which operate as cranes and conductors, transformers and classifiers under the direct command of the mind."

The elucidation could not be simpler; however, it still offered an opportunity for questions.

"Here then, do we encounter thought itself?" asked Hilario with great interest.

"Not exactly," answered the mentor. "Thought, which is created by each individual exclusively, flows incessantly from our cerebral field. It happens, similarly, with heat and magnetic waves that are unique to each of us. We constantly use our thought activating the resources we possess."

"It is not so easy to differentiate between the mental creation that comes from us and the one that comes from others and influences our brain," pondered my intrigued colleague.

"Your assertion lacks a sound base," exclaimed the mentor. "Any person who knows how to direct their attention will perceive the difference. Our thoughts vibrate at a unique frequency that reflects our habits and points of view, the mannerisms and the styles that are particular to us."

He then added good-humouredly:

"In matters of this type it is indispensable to be careful in our judgments. If we base our criterion on the measure of earthly expressions, our mental life is usually parasitical and restricted. Instead of using our ability to reflect, we act with prejudice or with pragmatic pre-established customs. The styles of the day and purely formal opinions that we effortlessly embrace also influence us. It is enough, however, to practice meditation and continue studying in order to discern the quality of our thoughts. This will help us to clearly identify the spiritual energies that we assimilate."

Hilario thought for a few moments. The satisfaction reflected in his face was of someone who has made an important discovery and he said quite pleased:

"Now I can conceive how mediumistic phenomenon can happen in simple situations as much as in the notable deeds of excellence."

"Yes," the mentor agreed, preoccupied with the length of our conversation. "Mediumship is a gift intrinsic to all souls, just as is the faculty of breathing, and each person assimilates the superior or inferior forces with which he or she is in tune. For this reason, Jesus recommended prayer and vigilance, so that we do not fall victims to the suggestions of evil. Temptation is the fluid of live forces that we radiate. Upon reaching similar elements, these forces weave a thick net of impulses around our soul that sometimes become irresistible."

Then, looking ahead to his next tasks, he added:

"Let us study as we work. The time utilized in service of our neighbor is a blessing in our own behalf that we will treasure forever."

6

Conscious Trance Communication[4]

The services in the Spiritist Center were proceeding harmoniously. Three spiritual guards entered the room escorting an unfortunate brother who was ready to receive the group's assistance.

It was an unhappy discarnate unmarried man who could not make sense of where he was. He did not know who was escorting him and he was disoriented, as if he had suddenly lost his ability to see and hear.

---

[4] **N.T.:** Also known as psychophony (it can be either conscious or unconscious).

"He is an obsessor who has recently left an ambient he knew for a long time," said Aulus compassionately.

"He died in his prime after extenuating himself in wild festivity. A lethal intoxication reduced his body to a cadaverous state. He lacked the slightest interest in seeking out the truths of the spirit."

And, as if aware of the previously prepared assistance being offered, Aulus continued:

"Observe. This is someone who acts within his own gloomy sphere. He was brought to this room by a route unknown to him, as is done with any patient with a serious mental condition. His distressed mind is confused by passion for a particular woman and he continues to drain energy from her physical body. This woman today is a tortured person who has been attuned to him to the point of retaining him at her side amidst tears and afflictions. He is disoriented by the loss of his physical body and with his spiritual deficiency he is like a person shipwrecked in a storm.

"Meanwhile, adapting himself to the physical body of the woman whom he loved, he found in her a new instrument for his sensations: seeing through her eyes, listening through her ears, often speaking through her voice, and vitalizing himself through the food she ingested. They have lived like this for almost five years. But now the perturbed and undernourished young lady is suffering significant organic imbalances.

"Because the sick woman requested our assistance, we were obliged to perform a double rescue. He feels fear facing the reality of the spirit-world. She is assaulted by his phobias and needs help to remove the energies that surround her. Just as a tree constrained by a parasitic plant needs cleaning, she needs to be free from him to restore her health."

Meanwhile, the spiritual guards obeyed Clementino and brought the patient next to Eugenia. The mentor of the Center approached Eugenia and applied strong magnetic energy over her cerebral cortex, after projecting numerous beams of luminous rays over an extensive area of the glottis.

We saw Eugenia-Spirit move away from her body and stay a few inches from it. The visitor, aided by the friends who guided him, sat close-by and leaned toward the medium with the attitude of someone looking out a window.

Viewing that picture, I recalled the activities of the vegetable kingdom wherein one plant is united with another. I concluded that such an association could be compared to a subtle process that grafts the neural system of the medium with the patient's mind.

The medium at first seemed agitated, but relaxed after a sighing a few times. I observed that a few brilliant threads were connecting Eugenia's forehead, who was detached from her body, with the brain of the communicating Spirit. As I directed a questioning look at Aulus, he immediately explained:

"It is the phenomenon of conscious psychophony or trance communication mediumship. Although he uses Eugenia's forces, the sick Spirit is controlled by her nervous magnetic energy, through which our sister is informed of the words he intends to say. He has taken temporary possession of our sister's vocal cords and senses, thereby managing to discern, listen and reason with a certain amount of equilibrium through her energies. Eugenia, however, firmly controls the reigns of her will, operating as if she were a benevolent nurse helping a patient by agreeing with his requests. Yet she sets a limit on his desires because, conscious of the intentions of the unfortunate companion to whom she lends her physical body, she reserves the right to correct any undesirable conduct.

"As his mental impulses reverberate in her thoughts through her nervous system's magnetic current, she acknowledges the words as they are formed and evaluates them before he speaks. She can thereby interrupt any abuse by analyzing his objectives and expressions. The entity is disturbed and suffering, and, being inferior to her, Eugenia does not descend to his level in order to help him.

"Every perturbed Spirit is mentally impaired and requires assistance. In charity sessions such as this, the first rescuer is the medium that connects with it. If the medium falls to the vibratory level of the one seeking help, there is little hope for an effective rescue. When the medium is aware of one's responsibilities, one is obliged to collaborate in assisting the discarnates. Thus, one will permit a free manifestation only to the point that it is not contrary to the harmony of the group and the dignity of the Center."

"Then," added Hilario, "in such tasks, the medium is never very far from one's own body."

"Yes. When the task involves disturbed entities, it is dangerous for the medium to be too far away. If we make a long trip, we feel safe when we leave conscientious and responsible friends to guard our home. In rendering assistance to disturbed brothers, we do not have this security and so our presence is imperative."

Eugenia was preoccupied and vigilant, remaining close to the sick one, who was commencing to speak through her. Aulus said:

"If needed, our friend can return to her body instantly. They are both momentarily joined in a union in which the communicator represents the action, but the medium personifies the will. In all fields of endeavor it is natural for the superior to be dominant over the inferior."

At that moment, the Spirit who was the cause of our attention, put his hand over his face in a gesture of relief and exclaimed in astonishment:

"I can see! I can see! But what enchantment ties me down? What chains hold me to this heavy body? What is the purpose of this silent and somber assembly? Who brought me here? Who brought me here?"

We perceived that Eugenia, still apart from her physical body, was monitoring to the words flowing from her mouth, her vocal cords temporarily used by the pilgrim of the shadows. She seemed to automatically store them firmly in her memory.

"The patient," said the mentor, "upon making contact with the nervous forces of the medium, revives his own senses. This dazzles him. He complains about the chains that bind him. These chains are fifty percent the result of Eugenia's cautious actions. As a result, he conducts himself as someone completely out of his mind, but under control. This is indispensable to the success of the rescue task."

"What if our sister lacked this authority?" Hilario was curious.

"She could not lend him assistance, as she would then be on the same level as he," our mentor clarified calmly.

With an inspired image to illustrate the problem, he added:

"A passive medium in such circumstances can be compared to a surgical operating table on which the sick patient is restricted for medical assistance. If this table were not firm or have the required supplies, any intervention would be impossible."

"But does our friend see the Spirit which she received in her physical body as clearly as we do?" I asked.

"In Eugenia's case, this does not occur," explained Aulus, amicably, "because her efforts to protect her personal energies, along with her interest in assisting to the best of her ability, do not allow her to focus her entire vision on his outer form. However, the afflictions and pains of the rescued one are reproduced in her; she feels his pain and his excitement, registering his suffering and his discomforts."

As Aulus was talking, the communicating Spirit exclaimed:

"Are we, by chance, facing a tribunal? What is this strange reception and why am I here at such an inopportune moment? I warn you that no one offends me, Liborio dos Santos, without suffering retaliation.

And, as if his inner conscience were torturing him, he frantically yelled.

"Who accuses me of despoiling my mother and abandoning her? I cannot be held responsible for the trials of others. Am I not in more pain than she is?"

At this instant, Hilario looked at the obsessor with compassion and respect, asking:

"Could his ailments simply be the result of moral anguish?"

"Not completely," declared Aulus. "Moral crisis may affect the perispirit. The brother whom we are currently treating has a lacerated perispiritual brain and the scourge that invades his fluidic body is as authentic as that of an incarnate person suffering from an intracranial tumor."

Displaying great interest in the study, Hilario persisted:

"Could incarnates question him on the spiritual life? Would he be able to explain himself?"

Aulus shook his head slightly, saying:

"Not in his condition. The treatment we offer is a charity, but one crucial for life itself. It would be fruitless to try to verify any hypothesis by questioning him. He is mentally impaired and, for a time, experiences lesions in his centers of reasoning.

"He takes with him the inheritance of a disturbed existence. He is attracted to the woman who loves him, yet he persecutes her, wanting only a parasitic life that absorbs and feeds on her energy. He enfolds her in sickly fluids and depends on her in the way a climbing vine extends and proliferates over a wall. Considering the shock produced by his death, we cannot expect him to give us a satisfactory and complete personal identification."

Meanwhile, Liborio continued, very disturbed.

"Who could withstand this situation? Is someone hypnotizing me? Who is controlling my thoughts? Of what good is it to restore my sight if you tie down my arms?"

Observing him compassionately, the mentor informed us:

"He is complaining about being controlled by Eugenia's will."

Thinking about the questions that were burning in our souls, Hilario objected:

"While in a state of consciousness and hearing the words from the communicating Spirit who uses her vocal cords, it is possible that Mrs. Eugenia is affected by great doubts. Could she believe that the words she is uttering are her own? Could she experience these hesitations?"

"It is possible," agreed the mentor; "although, our sister is capable of perceiving that the turmoil and the words spoken are not hers."

"But, if doubt did overcome her?" continued the colleague.

"Then," Aulus said courteously, "her own mind would reject it and expulse the communicating Spirit, annulling a precious opportunity for service. Doubt, in this case, would be a crystallized wave of negative forces."

Because Raul Silva was initiating the conversation with the rebellious guest, the friendly mentor invited us to observe.

7

Spiritual Rescue

Silva stood and, under Clementino's influence, which enveloped him completely, directed himself to Liborio, saying kindly:

"My friend, let us stay calm and ask for divine guidance."

"I am sick. Desperately sick."

"Yes, but even in sickness we should not lose our confidence. We are children of our celestial Father who is generous with His love."

"Are you a priest?"

"No, I am your brother."

"You lie. I do not even know you."

"We are all one family under God."

The perturbed questioner started laughing, and said:

"You must be a fanatic priest to speak in such terms."

The patience of the counselor surprised us. He was not treating Liborio as if he were an inhabitant of the shadows, and this awakening in him an undignified curiosity.

Notwithstanding the valuable aid of the mentor who accompanied him, Raul Silva himself expressed compassion and fatherly interest. He received the guest without the slightest disturbance or irritation, just as he would a disturbed family member that returned home.

Perhaps for this reason the obsessor's anger lessened. As soon as the patient began to understand better the director of the group, we observed that Eugenia acquired renewed vigor in providing assistance.

"I am not a religious minister," continued Raul calmly, "but I would like you to accept me as your friend."

"What a laugh! Friends do not exist in moments of misery. Every companion I ever knew abandoned me. The only one left is Sara. I will never leave her."

Then he assumed an expression of someone

reminiscing about the person he was referring to, and added with indignation:

"I cannot understand the reason why you are obstructing my movements. That is useless. On the other hand, I do not know the reason that I contain myself. Any person that has been provoked to the extent that I have should have come to blows with all of you. What are these silent gentlemen and women doing here? What do you intend to do with me?"

"We are praying for your serenity," said Raul with a kind and endearing tone.

"What a novelty! What do we have in common? Do I owe you anything?"

"On the contrary!" explained the counselor firmly. "We are the ones who owe you our attention and assistance. We are in an institution of fraternal service and in it, as in a hospital, no one questions who is knocking at the door. Nor does it matter what particular problems he or she has because, above all, it is the obligation of Medicine and nursing to treat the bleeding wounds."

Following this exchange, conducted with sincerity and simplicity, Liborio appeared more pacified. Emissions of mental energy from Raul reached the obsessed sufferer's thorax, as if searching for his heart.

Liborio made an attempt to speak, but he was moved by the unexpected tenderness, as a traveler in the desert welcomes the fresh water of an oasis. Surprised, he found that his words were caught in his throat.

Inspired by Clementino, the counselor spoke with affection.

"Liborio, my dear brother."

These four words were pronounced with such a fraternal emotion that the guest could not contain the tears that sprang from the depths of his soul. Raul leaned over and raised his hands above him, transmitting a luminous magnetic discharge, saying:

"Let us pray."

After a moment of silence, the voice of the director of the Center, under Clementino's inspiration, prayed tenderly.

"Divine Master Jesus, please direct your compassionate eyes on our family united here.

Travelers from many pilgrimages rest at this moment under the blessed tree of prayer and we implore You to help us. We are Your servants, subordinate to Your infinite kindness, offering ourselves as Your imperfect workers.

Although You pray for us all, we ask a special blessing for the companion You sent to us. He is as a little lamb rejoining the fold or a blood brother returning home.

Lord, grant us the happiness to receive him with

open arms. Seal our lips so that we do not inquire about his origin, and open our souls for the opportunity of having him with us in peace. Lend inspiration to our words so that impudence does not find its way to our tongue, aggravating the inner wounds of our brother. Help us maintain the respect that we owe him.

Master, we are sure that chance does not operate in Your plans. Your love invariably reserves the best for us and daily brings us closer to necessary tasks. Our souls are strings of life in Your hands. Refine them so that we can obtain from on High the blessing of serving with You.

Our Liborio is another brother who has arrived from remote horizons of the past. Oh Lord, help us so that he does not find us pronouncing Your name in vain."

The visitor cried. We could see clearly that it was not the strength of the words that affected him, but rather the radiant feeling accompanying them. Raul Silva, under the blessed radiation of Clementino, appeared to be encircled by a ray of intense light.

"Dear God, what is happening to me?" shouted Liborio, face bathed in tears.

Brother Clementino signaled to one of the counselors of our plane. He produced a cloth screen measuring approximately one square meter, which appeared to be of sheer gauze and had distinctive controls.

Clementino maneuvered a small key in one of the corners of the apparatus and the material became covered in a light fluidic mass, white and vibratory. He immediately placed himself next to Raul, who under his control, said to the communicant:

"Remember my friend, remember! Try to recall. Watch the pictures that appear before your eyes."

Immediately, as if his attention had been compulsively drawn to the cloth screen, the visitor focused on it. From that moment on, we watched with surprise as the sensitized rectangle displayed various scenes in which Liborio himself was the principal protagonist. Receiving them mentally, Raul Silva, described them.

"Observe my friend, it is night. A confused murmur of voices is heard from afar. Your elderly mother is calling you to her bedside, asking for your assistance. She is exhausted. You are the only child she has left, her last hope in this tortured lifetime and her last hope for help. The poor lady is about to die. Her difficulty in breathing is torturing her. Her heart problem is foretelling the end of her body.

"She is afraid, fearful of being alone. It is Saturday during *Carnaval*,[5] and the neighbors have already departed for the festivity. She looks like a frightened child. She observes you anxiously and begs

---

[5]**N.T.:** Brazilian holiday festivity.

you to stay. You respond that you are leaving in just a few minutes, just enough time to bring her medication.

"You immediately walk to a piece of furniture in the adjacent room, and take the only money she has left, a few cruzeiros[6], which will allow you to enjoy that illusory happiness in the nightclub. The friendly Spirits of your home approach you, imploring you to help the patient who is close to death, but you appear to be impervious to all thoughts of compassion. You direct a few words hurriedly to your mother and depart for the street. In the public road, undesirable discarnate companions, with whom you have affinity, join you. Turbulent entities, hypnotized by vice, drag you from a slope.

"For three days and four nights you are totally given to madness, completely forgetful of your obligations. Only at dawn on Wednesday do you return, semiconscious and fatigued. The elderly lady, rescued by anonymous hands, no longer recognizes you. She awaits her death with resignation.

"You walk to a bedroom in the rear intending to refresh yourself by taking a bath. You open the gas key without lighting the heater and sit down for a few minutes. You are confused. Your body requires sleep after such a crazy exhaustion. Sleep comes over you.

---

[6]**N.T.:** Brazilian currency at the time this book was written. The currency in Brazil today is Real.

You fall asleep, half drunk, and the toxic gases kill you. On a sunny morning, the funeral car delivers you to the cemetery. Your death is considered a suicide."

At that moment, the interlocutor, as if waking from a nightmare, shouted desperately:

"Oh, that is the truth! The truth! Where is my home? Sara, Sara! I want to see my mother!"

"Calm yourself," counseled Raul compassionately, "we are never without divine assistance. Your home, friend, was closed along with your corporeal eyes. Your mother, now in other spiritual spheres, extends her loving and sanctifying arms to you."

The communicating Spirit was overcome with tears. This emotional crisis was so great that the spiritual mentor of the group rushed to remove him from the medium, entrusting him to the collaborators, so that he could be received and assisted in another organization nearby.

Liborio, having commenced the profound process of transformation, departed, and Eugenia returned to her normal state. The cloth used with the equipment once again resumed its original transparency, and I directed some improvised questions to the mentor.

"What function does that rectangle serve? What were those scenes that had instantaneously developed?"

"The apparatus," Aulus graciously informed us, "is a condenser of ectoplasm. It concentrates the rays of force projected by the participants of the meeting and reproduces the images that flow from the thoughts of the communicating entity. Not only does this occur for our observation, but also for analysis by the counselor, who receives the images in his intuitive field, aided by the magnetic energies from our plane."

"It is evident that the workings of such a machine must be marvelous!" – exclaimed Hilario, impressed.

"There is nothing strange about it," said the mentor. "The spiritual guest only perceived the reflections of his own mind, similar to a person who examines oneself through a mirror."

"But, if we are facing a condenser of forces," I pondered, "then the success of the task depends on the collaboration of every member of the group."

"Precisely!" confirmed the mentor. "The group of incarnates provide the ectoplasmic energy to those brothers that still find themselves semi-materialized in the vibratory stages of physical experience. For that very reason, Silva and Clementino require the cooperation of the entire group for the service to function harmoniously.

"Individuals that outwardly reveal undignified sentiments greatly perturb these functions. They cast into the condenser the shadows that they generate and interfere with the efficiency of the reunion. They impede the clear image on the cloth screen projected by the entity requiring comprehension and light."

Innumerable questions came to mind, but our mentor looked at us discreetly, as if to ask for our silence and attention.

8

Unconscious Trance Communication

A Spirit crossed over the threshold of the room, accompanied by a revered friend, an apostolic soul. The poor Spirit reminded me of a nobleman of long ago. He looked, however, as if he had come from the bowels of Earth. The fluids that covered him formed a dark, glutinous mass over his clothing, emitting a nauseating odor. Compared to the suffering entities before us, he was a horrendous sight.

Almost all of the different entities in the area reserved for the sick displayed masks of suffering, slightly eased by the expressions of repentance, faith, humility and hope. But on this horror-producing face that appeared to have emerged from a marsh moor, was added a countenance cold, perverse, astute and rude.

Because of the expression he wore when he suddenly appeared, even the most perturbed Spirits backed away. In his right hand, the recently arrived stranger carried a whip, which he intended to wield at the same time that he uttered boisterous exclamations.

"Who brought me here against my will?" he bellowed. "Cowards! Why have you brought me here? Where are the vultures that devoured my eyes? Despicable! You will pay dearly for the abuses that I have suffered."

And displaying the depth of his mental imbalance, he continued in an obstreperous tone:

"Who said that the insane revolution of the French would have repercussions in Brazil? The madness of one people cannot extend throughout the Earth. The privileges of nobility cannot be violated! They belong to the kings, who are undisputedly selected by God. We shall defend our prerogative to exterminate the propaganda of the rebels and murderers of kings.

"I will sell my slaves that know how to read. There will be no more pamphlets or commentaries on the rebellion. How can they produce without the lash of the whip on their backs? Captives will remain captives, gentlemen as gentlemen, and all the fugitives and criminals shall feel the weight of my wrath. I shall kill without pity. Give me five whipping posts. That is what I require to regain our tranquility. "

"He was a cruel land owner," clarified our friendly guide. "He died during the last days of the eighteen century but still maintains the forcefulness of his own selfishness. He cannot perceive anything except the pictures he created of his slaves as well as the wealth and the revenues of his former rural property. His thoughts are buried there and he haunts the reincarnated souls who were dear to him in colonial Brazil. Although we welcome him as a brother, we can declare that he was nothing more than a cruel executioner of the unfortunate captives that fell under his iron hand. His legion of servants felt first hand his tyrannical perversity over their own flesh."

Taking advantage of the spontaneous pause, I looked at the sad face of this recently arrived Spirit and observed that his eyes were feline and glassy, as if all the life had gone out of them. I was going to examine those inexpressive orbits more closely when the mentor, guessing my impulse, added:

"He hated the workers that escaped his grasp and when he was able to imprison them once again, he not only tied them to the whipping post, but made an example of them by burning out their eyes. Of the few black fugitives that resisted death, some were sentenced to be eaten alive by wild dogs. With such a system of repression he created terror, drawing to himself fame and fortune. In death, however, he encountered only hatred in the form of terrible persecutors.

"Many of his victims with tender souls forgave his offense, but some could not find the strength for an immediate pardon. The latter became avengers of their past, inflicting him with torturous fear. Entangled by usury and believing only in the power of gold, he did not realize that he was transported from one form of life to the other through death.

"He believes that he is in a prison of shadows tormented by slaves, a prisoner of his own victims. He finds himself torn between despair and remorse, tortured by the memory of the flagellations that he decreed, and hypnotized by the avengers of the present whom he had in the past executed. He lives in total blindness, due to the imbalance in his perispiritual body's visual ability."

While we reflected on this description, the unfortunate one was placed at Celina's side. This affected me unfavorably. Why should Celina, the best medium in the group, be chosen to receive such an undignified communicant?

I observed her luminous aura, which greatly contrasted with the pestilent attire of the stranger, and I was overwhelmed by an uncontainable fear. Would such an act not be similar to allowing a fine harp to be scratched or clawed by the paws of an animal? But Aulus quickly explained:

"Be calm. Our disturbed friend came to this temple under the supervision and with the consent of the mentors of the Center. There is no reason for fear, because deleterious fluidic emanations[7] recede instinctively before the spiritual light that neutralizes or disintegrates them.

"Each medium possesses his own personal ambient and each group is characterized by a particular magnetic energy that preserves and defends it. Infectious clouds from Earth are extinguished and fought by solar radiations, and deleterious fluidic emanations are either annihilated or swept away from the planet by the Spirit's superior energy. The luminous rays from a sound mind oriented toward goodness pass over evil similar to electric discharges. Aware that the most qualified will be more helpful, our sister Celina is the ideal companion for assistance at this time"

Gesturing toward her, he said: "Let us observe:"

The medium departed from her physical body as though yielding to a profoundly deep dream, taking with her the brilliant aura that crowned her. Clementino did not have to assist; Celina appeared accustomed to this type of task. Still feeling solicitous, he assisted her.

---

[7]**N.T.:** Fluidic (adj.) refers to fluid. By 'fluid" we denote not any kind of matter in particular; the word signifies an ethereal, undulating movement, analogous to those which cause electricity, light, heat, and X-rays.

The noble woman looked at the desperate visitor sympathetically and opened her arms to him, helping him to take possession of her now somewhat obscure physical body. As if drawn by a powerful magnet, the patient positioned himself over the physical body of the medium, instinctively uniting with her. Aided by the guardian who had had brought him, the patient sat down with difficulty. His mind appeared strongly attached to the brain of the medium.

Eugenia struck us as a meritorious nurse. Celina was more like a devoted mother, so affectionate was the attention she gave the patient. Brilliant threads that completely enfolded him emanated from her and, despite being his own master, the communicating Spirit became under her prudent control.

He, furiously and unsuccessfully, tried to escape, much as an animal trying to get free from a cage might. He projected gloomy rays, which mixed with the light of Celina-Spirit that affectionately enveloped him. He made an effort to protest with taunting remarks, but was unable to do so.

The medium was a passive instrument outwardly, but, in the depths of her being, held positive moral qualities that were her unalienable achievement. These impeded any dishonest conduct from this brother.

"I am Jose Maria..." shouted the irritated visitor, also mentioning other names with the obvious intent of giving greater importance to his origin. He issued claims and severe warnings, and rebelled with exasperation; however, I perceived that his language differed from that he had previously used. He appeared as if handcuffed and restrained; however he continued to be rude and gruff.

Soon, though, he appeared to adjust completely to the physiology of the medium. He now seemed so natural and spontaneous that I could not control the questions that rapidly came to mind. Was the trance mediumship of Celina different? If both Eugenia and she separated from their physical body during the work, why was the first one as preoccupied as a restless nurse, while the second one appeared to be like a devoted tutor to the demented brother, caring for him like a mother? Why does one appear tormented while the other appears serene and confident?

Mindful of our apprenticeship, Aulus began to explain while Clementino and Raul assisted the communicator by means of prayers and renovating phrases, which induced him toward goodness.

"Celina," he said, "is a perfect unconscious trance-communicating medium.[8] In her case, this takes place without the need to join the nervous energy of the mediumistic brain to the mind of the guest that occupies it. She concedes her resources to the entities so spontaneously that she has no difficulty in

---

[8]**N.T.:** Also known as a medium of psychophony (conscious or unconscious).

disassociating herself. This occurs automatically, causing her to momentarily lose contact with her brain's motor centers.

"Her mediumistic role is of extreme passivity. For this reason, the communicating entity manifests his own personality more accurately. This, however, does not imply that our sister is absent or irresponsible. Staying close to her body, she acts as a generous mother assisting the one in pain who is expressing himself through her, as if he were a fragile protégée of her kindness.

"She attracted him to her side by voluntary sacrifice, which is pleasing to her fraternal heart. The unfortunate Jose Maria, demented and immensely inferior to her, cannot reject her. He remains aggressive, but finds himself controlled by her superior mind. It is for this reason that the guest experiences the affectionate control of the missionary who protects him. Forced to obey, he receives her constricting mental energy, which coerces him to remain respectful despite his rebellion."

During a pause, we observed that Silva was progressing very well in his counseling. The former rural tyrant was starting to assimilate some of the luminous radiations. Hilario, notwithstanding, continued the instruction by asking:

"Even though we can see that she is a worthy assistant, could Celina recall the words spoken through her by the visitor?"

"If she so desired, she could remember them. But in this situation, she sees no advantage to retain or remember what she hears."

"Undoubtedly," posited my colleague, "we can observe a marked difference between the two mediums when in a trance. I believe that being a conscious trance medium, Eugenia exerts more direct control over the communicating Spirit. Celina, although watchful of the companion who is manifesting, allows him to act more voluntarily and with more liberty. But, if Celina were not a capable worker, being able to immediately intervene in any difficult circumstance, wouldn't the faculties of Eugenia be preferable?"

"Yes, Hilario, you are correct. Pure somnambulism can produce beautiful phenomenon, but is not too efficient in constructing spiritual goodness. Unconscious trance communication can be injurious to personal protection when used by those with insufficient moral values. Clear examples of this are the cases of spirit attachment that yield to vampirizing entities.

Hilario reflected for a moment, and then said: "Here we encounter the medium outside her physical body, mentally controlling an inferior entity. But what if it were the other way around? What if it were a Spirit of superior intellect who mentally controlled the medium?"

"In that case," the mentor expressed calmly, "Celina would be naturally controlled. Notwithstanding, if the communicant had a degenerate and perverse intelligence, the mentors of the Center would provide the necessary control. In the case of a messenger with an elevated knowledge and virtue, the medium would appear passive and pleased, much as rivers benefit by the rain that falls from above.

The mentor was going to continue, but Clementino asked his participation in the transfer of Jose Maria, who was starting to accept the service of the prayer, which brought tears of happiness to him. Once again entrusted to the paternal friend who had brought him in the Center, our mentor helped to assist the communicating Spirit in taking him to a distant rescue organization.

9

Possession

A small row of people came to seek assistance from the Center. One was a young man named Pedro. He appeared anguished, speaking words that I could not hear clearly. Brother Clementino, consulted by Aulus, told the mentor:

"Since today's activities are for study, we will permit the manifestation."

I realized that our mentor intended to let us witness an important demonstration. Invited by the instructor, we approached the young patient who was assisted by his gray-haired mother. On the supervisor's approval, the guards let an evidently mentally unstable

Spirit into the reunion. He suddenly crossed the safety lines that would normally prevent him from entering, frenetically shouting the young man's name.

His eyes were fixed on the patient; he observed nothing other than him. As he reached Pedro, our incarnate brother suddenly screamed and collapsed. The elderly woman rushed to break her son's fall.

Under the guidance of Clementino, Raul Silva quickly determined that the young man be isolated and brought to a bed in the adjoining room. Celina was put in charge. Along with her, we accompanied the patient with some concern.

In the room, various tasks continued without interruption while we got ready to provide the required treatment. Pedro and the obsessor that dominated him now appeared joined with one another. They were two contestants, intent on a fierce fight.

Pedro's collapse had all the classic symptoms of an epileptic attack. His face was transfigured by an indescribable paleness, his muscles contracted, his teeth clenched, and his head was flexed back. His arms flailed like two twigs of a tree in a storm.

Celina and the patient's loving mother helped to lay him on the bed. When they were about to pray, the rigidity of his body gave way to strange convulsions and his eyes rotated continuously. The pale face turned reddish like that which appears on congested faces. He had difficulty breathing and his sphincter relaxed. The insensitive persecutor appeared to have taken possession of the patient's body. Only we heard him speak harsh words as Pedro's sensory functions became inhibited.

Celina, caressing the patient, could sense both the gravity of the illness and the presence of the unfortunate visitor; however, she remained alert and ready to offer whatever assistance was needed. In vain, she tried to establish a communication with the executioner. He continued to scream, heedless of our pleas to remain calm.

"I will get even! I will get my revenge! I will extract justice with my own hands." He screamed angrily.

He would have said more injurious words but Pedro, still in convulsions, prevented him from using his vocal cords to pronounce them. The young man was completely linked to the executioner, who had suddenly taken control. His cerebral cortex appeared wrapped in a dark fluidic mass. We could recognize in the young man an evident incapacity to exercise control over himself. Aulus, caressing his perspiring forehead, expressed with obvious compassion:

"This is a case of complete possession manifested as epilepsy."

"Is our friend unconscious?" – asked Hilario with interest and respect.

"Yes, he is a sick terrestrial man who is, for now, without a connection to his carnal brain. The cells of the cortex are suffering an attack of toxic magnetic emissions. The motor centers are disorganized. The entire cerebellum is impregnated with deleterious fluids. The avenues of equilibrium appear completely perturbed.

"Pedro does not possess the means to govern himself, nor the awareness to register his own disquieting actions. This, however, occurs in the realm of dense matter, because in that of Spirit, he stores the particulars of his situation. This enriches the value of his experiences."

I observed the scene and, wanting to learn more, I asked:

"We are in the presence of an incarnate and a discarnate attached to one another. Notwithstanding their painful suffering, is it proper to describe this as a mediumistic trance?"

Without interrupting the assistance he was giving to Pedro, the mentor responded:

"Yes, this is an epileptic seizure according to the medical definition; however, it is also a minor mediumistic trance. The two unbalanced minds are strongly united by the hatred they feel for one another."

And, upon continuing his observance of the two unfortunates in convulsions, he added:

"Prior to the present reincarnation, which is a blessing for him, Pedro was in the lower zones. For many years, he and his adversary engaged in an ongoing duel in the purgatory zones. Today, the situation improved. Even though their encounters are less frequent, the young man's perispiritual body remains injured in critical areas."

Meanwhile, Celina found it difficult to reach the obsessor via the spoken word. Assisted by our mentor, she made an emotional prayer imploring divine compassion for the two unfortunate companions. The words of our venerable friend emitted vibrations of luminous forces that emanated from her hands and offered relief to the participants in the conflict.

As if he had breathed an anesthetic substance, the persecutor loosened himself from the victim, who then fell into a profound and restorative sleep. Guards and auxiliaries accompanied the slightly dazed obsessor to an isolated emergency room. And while Celina gave magnetized water to the patient's mother, who was still crying and frightened, we returned to our cordial conversation.

"In spite of the patient's condition, can we consider Pedro a medium?" – asked Hilario, expectantly.

"Due to the passiveness with which he receives his discarnate enemy, this idea is justifiable. We must consider, however, that above all he is a Spirit in debt who must redeem himself."

"But wouldn't he be able to face his own psychic development?"

The mentor smiled and observed:

"To develop means to improve, to increase, to intensify. Pedro must develop his personal resources through his spiritual improvement. Solid walls are not constructed over an insecure base. He will need, first of all, to cure himself. After this, then..."

"If this is so," objected my colleague, "won't his presence in this spiritist center be fruitless?"

"By no means. Here he will receive the strength to restore himself, just as fertilizer restores a scrawny plant. Day by day, in contact with friends oriented in the Gospel, he and his rival will assimilate valuable lessons and gradually modify their thinking. Once both personalities improve, the mediumistic faculty may then surface. As both sufferers absorb those healthy and renovating thoughts, they will improve. Since the thoughts of each act upon the other, this will intensify their recuperation."

Examining these complex problems, and noting our thoughtful attitude, the mentor continued:

"Valuable mediumistic gifts, naturally, are not improvised. They require great effort, sacrifice, will and time. And without love or dedication, the creation of meritorious mediumistic groups is not possible."

Returning his attention toward the sleepy patient, Aulus continued:

"Our friend is controlled by a significant number of debts from the past and it is divine law that no one can advance toward the future without paying them. Pedro's trials are expressed through his mediumship. For this reason, he should be treated as a sick person who requires warmth and assistance."

He immediately checked Pedro's forehead, as if desiring to retrieve the information needed to complete the lesson, and stood by him in careful observation. After a few moments of silence, he said:

"Although their struggle comes from deep in the past, we do not have sufficient time for a complete review. We can, however, immediately recognize the avenger of today as the victim of yesterday. During the middle of the last century, Pedro was a doctor who abused his mission to cure. An in-depth mental analysis would no doubt find him taking part in numerous dishonest ventures.

"The persecutor who today controls his personality was a former blood brother whose wife Pedro tried to seduce. To do this, he not only jeopardized his brother both in business and socially, he also succeeded in relegating him to a hospice. There his brother remained for years, confused and helpless, awaiting death.

"Upon discarnating, he found his brother with his wife. His distress turned to hate. He pursued them in life, waited for them beyond the tomb, where the three of them would reunite and initiate the anguishing process of regeneration.

"The wife, who had less culpability, was the first to return to the physical world. She received the former delinquent doctor as her own son, thereby purifying the love in her soul. The former brother who had been double-crossed did not have the strength to change and so he tortures Pedro, completely controlled by his hatred."

Responding with patience to our expression of amazement, he added:

"We live in the hell that we create for others. No one can elude justice. Reparations can be delayed, but they are inevitable."

The lesson was simple; we were amazed, however, by the terrible situation of the fatigued and sad patient. Always inquisitive, Hilario considered:

"If Pedro is a tortured medium, what could he accomplish in this group?"

The mentor smiled as he responded:

"Chance does not operate in superior designs. We do not meet each other without reason. Our friend most probably has affectionate ties from the past here and their duty is to assist him. If he cannot be of value to the group, he can and must receive the fraternal assistance imperative for his improvement and elevation."

"Will his cure be quick?" I inquired.

"Who could know that?" responded Aulus serenely. Weighing his words, he continued:

"That will depend upon him and his former victim. The assimilation of principles that restore good thoughts is crucial to a higher vision of life. All dark dramas of obsession are generated in disturbed minds. If he perseveres in applying himself sincerely to the consoling doctrine taught here, converting to goodness, it will surely shorten the length of his expiation. This will, in turn, change his adversary's mental state, who will be induced to improve by the exposure to his practice of renunciation, humility and faith.

"Even after the possession ends, Pedro will still suffer imbalances. Minor secondary epilepsy will emerge in him for some time by simply recalling the violent battles that he had sustained. Eventually, though, his whole perispiritual body will be readjusted."

"And will this task take long?" inquired Hilario quite affected.

Our mentor replied:

"Who can penetrate the conscience of others?

With the strength of the will it is possible to achieve the solution to many enigmas and lessen pain. The matter, however, is an intimate one. Let us be sure that the seeds of light are never lost. If the mediums going through tremendous trials today were to persist in cultivating better destinies, they would be transformed into valuable workers, which would bring about reincarnations of growth and progress."

And with our admiration, he concluded:

"The problem is to learn without becoming disillusioned and to serve without giving up."

10

Tortured Somnambulism

We returned to the room. Eugenia had just finished rescuing a poor brother who had recently died. He left the room under the fraternal control of the spiritual collaborators.

Clementino graciously received us. He led us to a young woman, one of a small group of patients that would be receiving assistance on that evening, who was praying devoutly. A distinguished gentleman accompanied her. Caressing her head, the mentor said:

"We will allow the manifestation of an unfortunate interfering companion, not only to rescue him but also for us to learn of tortured somnambulism."

The young lady bent toward the impeccably dressed man, who stood protectively at her side. The group's mentor withdrew to assist with other tasks under his direction. Aulus took his place and proceeded to explain this case with his characteristic kindness. Referring to the couple, he informed us:

"They are husband and wife, united to redeem a debt."

The spiritual guards permitted access to a crazed discarnate with a dense perispirit. He undoubtedly was bringing with him the stigma of mental alienation: an altered look, a fierce countenance, and an anxiety could not be hidden. His presence would inspire revulsion and terror in those less familiar with the treatment of these patients. In addition to a head injury, he had extensive ulcerations in his throat.

He approached the young female as a feline stalks his prey. The gentle woman began screaming, completely transformed; yet, she, in Spirit, did not separate from her body. She went into contortions, crying profusely, surrounded by the fluidic vibrations of the entity that completely oppressed her physiological field.

Tears flowed from her half-closed eyes. Her body appeared without control as a boat without a boatman and her breathing was erratic and labored. She made an effort to speak, but her voice was a disagreeable whistle. Her vocal cords were incapable of articulating an intelligible phrase.

Raul, under the direction of Clementino, applied magnetic energy over the medium's thorax and she then spoke in a clamorous nasal twang:

"Ungrateful daughter. Criminal! Criminal! Nothing will save you! You will descend with me into the dark shadows and share my pain. I do not want help. I want you to remain with me. I will not forgive you! I will not forgive you!"

From this convulsive crying he began laughing as one bent on revenge. Yet the laugh was such that we could not discern whether we were facing a victim in pain or a sarcastic clown.

"Justice is on my side," he screamed menacingly. "I am the attorney of my personal cause and vengeance is my only recourse."

Raul, inspired by his protecting Spirit, tried to change the tormentor's attitude by talking about the value of humility, forgiveness, understanding and love. While he continued counseling, we sought contact with our diligent mentor. Anticipating our first questions, Aulus emphasized:

"It is a painful case, one we see repeated in thousands of beings."

"We can see," exclaimed Hilario greatly impressed, "that it is our sister who is speaking and gesticulating."

"Yes," affirmed the mentor. "However, she finds her brain connected to that of the obsessing Spirit."

"Will she be able to recall clearly what is occurring now?" I inquired.

"Not at all! The unfortunate suffering friend disorganized the cells of her cerebral cortex. In trances in which there is a close union between her demented persecutor and herself, she enters a deep hypnosis. This is similar to what happens to people who are magnetized in demonstrations of hypnotism. The medium immediately shows the mental imbalances of the one manifesting."

And referring to the mediums' throat, suddenly reddish and inflamed, he continued:

"At this moment her glottis is controlled momentarily by his interference. She can only express herself in a coarse voice and broken words. This is because our tortured brother, to whom she is related by the most intimate ties, transmits his personal sensations through her."

"Their association seems to be so strong," declared Hilario, "that I must ask myself if they could be two souls occupying a single body, similar to two plants of different species growing in the same pot. Is it possible that our sister is oppressed by her tormentor in her daily life without being aware of it?"

"Your thinking is correct. The young woman is an enigma to her family. She has a notable background and possesses refined cultural traits; her conduct, however, is obstinate, revealing hidden imbalances and irregularities.

"Since her teens, she manifested dissatisfaction and melancholia, causing nervous and circulatory problems. Renowned doctors tried in vain to diagnose her condition. One surgeon believed that the problem was a thyroid dysfunction and submitted her to a delicate surgery, but her ailments continued.

"Later, she wed the gentleman who accompanied her here today. He was convinced that matrimony would constitute a healthful change for her, but her situation only worsened.

"In time, she became pregnant. In a plan designed in the superior world, our sister should receive as her child the one who now persecutes her. She was to assist in his transformation and aid him in achieving a new destiny. Sensing his proximity, however, she became terrified and refused to follow through with this pre-assigned task. Impervious to the council of her own soul, she had an abortion.

"This act resulted in a greater influence in her married life from the invisible adversary. She suffered hysterical crises and displayed a sudden aversion to her husband. At night, in particular, she suffered suffocating and anguishing attacks, embittering her desolate husband. Many doctors were consulted, but the sedatives and narcotics were of no use.

"Dominated by these disorders, the patient was put in an institution. There, neither medicine nor electroshock therapy resolved her problem. She is now at home with her family for a period of rest. Her husband is considering Spiritism to assist in alleviating her illness."

While Silva and Clementino attempted to calm the medium and the communicant, Hilario and I continued avidly to seek greater clarification.

"Could she become pregnant again?" – inquired my colleague.

"Yes," Aulus assured us calmly, "and this would be a blessing for her. Her conflict, however, prevents her from attending to her obligations, so she cannot conceive just now."

I recalled the woman who gave birth in hospices, but upon perceiving my thoughts, the mentor explained:

"Her mental alienation does not deprive her of nature's blessings, but she rebelled against her obligations and this caused genetic imbalances. Our most intimate faults, although unknown by others, jeopardize our subtle nature and prevent our healing, though remorse helps to begin restoring our good intentions. The perfect interlocking of the psychophysical elements is based in the mind. Corporeal life is the synthesis of radiations of the soul. There is no organic harmony in our organs without balanced thoughts, just as there is no order without intelligence."

The spiritual assistance continued with hopeful expectation. The vengeful Spirit attached to the medium remained under the control of Clementino's advisors. At the same time, the young lady reflected her tormentor's emotions and impulses. She had palpitations in her chest and lamented tearfully:

"For me there is no aid. I am a renegade."

"Be forgiving, dear brother, and the panorama will change you," replied Raul, affectionately. "When we forgive, we are forgiven. We all have debts. Will you not help others so that you too might also be assisted?"

"I cannot," cried the unfortunate one, "I cannot."

Acknowledging the pair of suffering Spirits in the same physical body, Aulus continued his explanation:

"When observing the harshness of obsession in a tortured mediumship, we must not forget that the causes of today's suffering have their roots in yesterday. The Spiritist Centers are replete with moving dramas, vehicles of the remote past and the immediate present."

And referring to the couple with his hand, he continued:

"Today's husband was in the past a harmful companion to our obsessed sister. He persuaded her to poison her adoptive father and today her victim pursues her.

"She lived last century in an aristocratic mansion and was legal heir to a considerable fortune. The opulent widower who had raised her with loving care was not in favor of her matrimonial selection. The young man appeared more interested in taking control of her finances than in bringing happiness to the unsuspecting and inexperienced young girl. He was unable, however, to draw her away from the young man. Indignant, he commenced legal measures to disinherit her.

"The young man exploited the young girl's passion and induced her to eliminate the father by giving him continuous doses of narcotics. Extremely debilitated after two weeks of imbibing incorrect medication, it took only a minute dose of corrosives for death to come. After a short period of mourning, the young couple married and the husband assumed control of her inheritance.

"In a short time, however, she was filled with afflictive disillusions. Her husband was a compulsive gambler and a libertine, which caused her to undergo profound moral and physical misery. The gradual annihilation was not enough to rid herself of the discarnated tutor. He attached himself to her with the ardent desire for vengeance, causing her horrible torment.

"Earthly society ignored the murder but it was registered in the divine tribunals, giving origin to a long process of attonement that still continues today. We are observing here the trio of consciences bound by fibers that will loosen only through redemption."

The unfortunate persecutor received the affectionate teachings from Raul Silva and, after a brief interval, the mentor continued:

"Our sister's tragedy originates in the past. In the inferior planes of spiritual life, she withstood the hatred of her victim, who transformed himself into her vengeful creditor. Nowadays, in her present reincarnation, he followed her thoughts as she went from infancy to puberty under his hidden influence.

"When his enemy from the past became her husband again in this life, with the intent of helping and reeducating her, in addition to the weakness showed by our friend in her first attempt of motherhood, the obsessing Spirit took advantage of the magnetic influence that he exercised over her and broke down her equilibrium."

Moved by the justice playing out before us, we could not avoid further questioning. Turning the attention to the victim's husband who supported her affectionately, Hilario considered:

"In other words, our friend has his own debt to resolve along with his sick wife."

"Without a doubt," Aulus confirmed in a grave tone. "Divine power does not place us close to another without just cause. In marriage, home or work, we are sought out for our affinity to satisfy the imperatives of the law of love. This occurs whether to bring about good or to clear debts we have accrued during our prior deliberate evil actions.

"Our sister suffers the effects of her crime because of her intense desire to enjoy the pleasures that disrupted her consciousness. Her former husband inspired this deplorable action. This same Spirit is her husband in this life and assists her in making amendments."

I looked at the depressed gentleman, who appeared as if he considered his frustration as permanent. My simple reflection was sufficient for the mentor to explain, solicitously:

"It is true, our friend is not happy. He married his wife from the past seeking to renew the prior passionate adventures with her, but instead he found the sick woman we see here. This is the cause of his suffering."

"Notwithstanding, is she acting as a medium?" – Hilario asked.

"Of course, she is a medium in the afflictive process of clearing a debt.

"It is probable that she will need affection and love for a few years. Still caught in the fluidic nets of her demented adversary, she will become purified through the pain and as a result of her tortured somnambulism. She will put the patience and goodwill of this group of workers to the test. There is, however, no prospect of an immediate achievement, as she is still in extreme need of fraternal aid."

"Naturally," I added, "her presence here shall not be in vain."

"In no way," added the mentor. "First of all, she and her husband constitute a valuable nucleus in which our companions in service may improve their qualifications as sowers of the light. In addition to this, the fruits of the counseling will not be lost. At night, reunion after reunion, in prayer and constructive observations, the trio of souls will slowly become renewed. The persecutor will understand that to better himself he must forgive; the patient will recuperate by strengthening herself in Spirit; and the husband will find genuine happiness as he acquires patience and calm."

At this point the persecutor, with the cooperation of the spiritual friends of the Center, was separated from the psychic ambient of the young lady and she returned to normal. Then, kindly answering our questions, the mentor added:

"When our brother Clementino asked us to observe this case, he undoubtedly wanted us to see how work, tolerance, comprehension and kindness build and maintain an efficient mediumship in the world. Mediums appear all over; however, a rare few have already liberated themselves from their somber past to serve humanity in the present. No one advances and acquires serenity without paying the tribute they owe from their past. Therefore, may we be granted the ability to tolerate difficulties, to be helpful to others and to build our deeds on goodness."

Our conversation was interrupted. Clementino, ever diligent, was calling to us to cooperate in other tasks.

11

Out-of-Body Experience in Service

It was time for Antonio Castro's to use his mediumship. Profoundly focused, he demonstrated the confidence of one wholly dedicated to the task. Brother Clementino, using his magnetic ability, placed his hands over him and applied longitudinal passes.

Castro slowly fell asleep while his arms tensed and turned rigid. From his thorax emanated an abundant cloudlike whitish vapor, rapidly transforming itself on his left side as a duplicate but somewhat larger figure of the medium. Our friend appeared with all his physical characteristics appreciably enlarged.

I wanted to ask a few questions, but the solemnity of the service required silence. The spiritual director of the Center was submitting the medium to a delicate magnetic intervention that should not be interrupted.

The medium took a few steps from his disassociated body, leaving the silver cord[9] that bonded him to his somatic field. While his physiological body rested, Castro came close to us stuttering and surprised, appearing as a strange replica of himself. He appeared larger; his right side was bluish and his left side orangish. He tried to move but he appeared to feel heavy and uncomfortable.

Clementino repeated his magnetic operations and Castro, out-of-body, positioned himself to re-enter his body. Then I saw that, from this a singular difference resulted. The corporeal body instinctively absorbed a certain amount of force, which was causing an irregularity in his perispirit in a manner incomprehensible to me. From that instant, the medium, outside of his dense physical body, preserved the appearance that was characteristically his own.

He was once again himself without any distortion, light and agile, although he remained bound to his physical body through the silver cord. As

---

[9]**N.T.:** Silver Cord: the link between the spiritual and the physical body. When the cord is broken, the physical body dies, and the Spirit is free to continue life in the spirit-world.

Castro-Spirit moved about in our area, the cord appeared finer and more luminous. While Clementino comforted him with friendly words, our mentor noticed our curiosity and quickly explained to us:

"With the supervisor's assistance, the medium was disassociated from his body. At first, his perispirit or *astral body*, was recharged by vital emanations that control the equilibrium between the soul and the corporeal body. This is known as the *etheric double*, which is formed by neuro-psychic emanations that belong to the physiological field. For this reason, it cannot achieve a greater separation from the physical body. The *etheric double* also suffers disintegration at death.

"To better adjust to our ambient, Castro returned these energies to his motionless body, thereby warming it. This liberated him as much as possible so that he could perform the service that awaited him."

"Ah!" – said Hilario with admiration – "here we see the outward expression of sensitivity."

"Yes. If a human investigator were to injure the medium's perispiritual body, our friend would immediately register the pain of that blow. He could verbalize the injury to his perispirit through his vocal cords because his body is connected to them via the silver cord.

I observed Castro attentively. He was not dressed in the grayish-blue suit that he had been wearing, but rather in a long white robe that fell from his shoulders to the floor. The robe obscured his feet and he moved about as if he were gliding. Aulus noticed my close observations and clarified:

"With the help of Clementino, Castro is utilizing his ectoplasmic forces, which are increased by our ambient. Our soul emits this energy according to the density of our corporeal organization, varying from luminescent radiations to pasty substances, as the diverse phenomena of metamorphosis take place in a chrysalis.

After watching the hesitant medium for a few moments, he continued:

"Castro is still a novice in this service. As he gains more experience, he will be able to handle more advanced mental possibilities, since the perispirit is molded by thought. This occurs whether the thoughts arise from our imagination or from intelligences more vigorous than ours, and particularly when our will surrenders unconsciously to tyrannical or vicious Spirits.

"Our friend, then, if he could..." – began Hilario with curiosity. Interrupting him, the mentor continued:

"If, while outside the physical field, he were to focus and exercise self-control, he could control the plastic forces and could present and dress himself in any form he wanted and that would please us."

"Yet," I wondered, "this form, although alive, is not comparable to the clothes of the spiritual plane... "

Aulus perceived from my comment that I desired greater clarification for Hilario's sake, who was still a novice in our field. Aulus cooperated and tried to clarify:

"Yes. Our thoughts indicate the various forms that each of us wants to adopt, although our instruments of presentation in the spiritual sphere where we live, as you have already known, will vary in many ways. We could liken this to a tattooed man. He chooses a design that is attractive to him and others recognize him by that design. Yet, he also covers the tattoo with clothes that please him and conform to his milieu."

And smiling, he added:

"Through mental concentration, any Spirit can display the expression he desires. Using our creativity, we can mobilize the resources available to us. This helps us perfect artistic concepts we have with our common relations. Our art and science is much richer than in the circle of incarnates. Because of this, all education develops more efficiently.

"We are unable to conceive of a dignified and noble terrestrial society that practices nudism, even if they are exquisitely tattooed. Likewise, individuals in our community may have a prodigiously sculptured body engraved by mental forces, yet use clothes to express esthetic taste. Progress is an educational task. Our spiritual ascent is not possible if we regress to the empiricism characteristic of a tribal era."

Aulus became silent. The medium, more at ease outside of the dense physical body, received Clementino's paternal instructions. Two collaborators placed a helmet over his head that acted as a pair of blinders.

"Being inexperienced at this type of task," the mentor told us, "Castro should not become distracted. He requires adequate means for inhibiting his own observations so as to interfere as little as possible."

We saw the young man outside of his body, rising in space, and grasping the hands of both assistants. The trio ascended in a slanted position as we expected. From that moment forth, demonstrating a clear communion with his corporeal body, we heard him speak:

"We are following a dark and narrow path! Oh I am afraid! Very fearful! Rodrigo and Sergio are protecting me on this journey but I am afraid. I have the sense of being in total darkness."

He expressed anguish and fear as he continued:

"What kind of darkness is this? It is a weight on us. Oh dear, oh dear! I see unknown forms moving under our feet. I want to return! I cannot continue. I cannot stand it. I cannot stand it!"

However, Raul, inspired by the mentor of the Center, raised the vibratory level of the group as he formulated a fervorous prayer in which he begged the Almighty to give more strength to Castro. Close to us, Aulus explained:

"The prayer from the group reaches him and acts as a spiritual tonic."

"Ah! Yes! My friends," continued Castro, as if his physical body were a radio apparatus for distant communications. "Your prayers acted upon me as if they were a rainfall of light. I appreciate the benefits. I feel comforted! I will continue ahead!"

Interpreting the processes that we had observed, the mentor explained:

"Very rarely do incarnate Spirits achieve absolute control over themselves outside their body. Accustomed to the physical organism, when facing any unpleasant surprise in this unaccustomed sphere, they instinctively try to return to their corporeal body, just like the mollusk that seeks refuge within its shell. Castro, on the other hand, shall be taught to lend valuable assistance to the patients whatever their condition."

While the mentor made these observations, the medium's voice filled the entire room, loud and clear.

"What a relief! We broke through the barrier of the darkness! This atmosphere is perfumed with a delicate aroma! The stars are once again shining brilliantly. Oh! It is a city of light... Brilliant towers are standing up the sky! We are now entering a great park! Oh my God! Who do I see smiling at me? It is our Oliveira! How different he is, much younger, much much younger!" Abundant tears bathed the face of the medium, affecting all of us. With the gesture of one who is lovingly embracing another heart to heart, the medium continued:

"What happiness! What happiness! Oliveira my friend, I have missed you so much! Why haven't we been receiving your cooperation? We know that God's will must prevail, but to be away from you has been a torment for us. The memory of your love still lives in our circle. Your work remains an unforgettable example of Christian love! Please return! Return to stimulate us in the seedbed of goodness. Beloved friend, although we know that death is the true life, we feel your loss."

Painful sobbing cut off our traveler's voice, which could be heard from a great distance. Our own Raul was equally moved to tears. Aulus explained what was occurring:

"Oliveira had been an untiring worker in this evangelical sanctuary. He died a few days ago and Castro, with the consent of the guides of this Center, went to give him an affectionate greeting from all of his co-workers. He remains there in order to renew himself, as he is not yet capable of a more direct communication with the brothers left behind. But he will be able to send a message through Castro."

"Embrace me, yes, dear friend!" continued Castro with an indescribable inflexion of fraternal warmth. "Here I am. I will relay anything you wish. Speak, and I will repeat it!"

Then, assuming the position of one who must appear as a dignified intermediary, he modified his facial expressions while speaking rhythmically for his listeners:

"Dear friends, may God repay you. I am well, but convalescing and incapable of completing such a tiring trek. I feel comforted, almost happy. Undoubtedly, I do not merit the blessings received, as I see myself in a grand home, under the protection of unforgettable and sublime affections. The prayers said by our group reach me nightly as a projection of flowers and blessings!

"How can I express my gratitude, since the earthly word is always insufficient in defining the great sentiments of our life? May the Father repay you all! Here I have come to realize once again of what little value I am. Now I can affirm that all of our sacrifices for the cause of the righteousness are mere trifles compared to the magnificence of the Divine kindness! My dear friends, charity is the divine path. Let us give service! May Jesus bless all of us!"

Castro's voice was silenced and a few minutes later we saw him re-entering his carnal body with ease, assisted by the brothers who had led him there.

Strangely trying to accommodate himself, as if the physical body had absorbed him unexpectedly, he awoke in the carnal sphere. He was once again in possession of his normal faculties, rubbing his eyes, as would anyone after a long sleep.

The out-of-body experience in service had concluded. We all had received a valuable lesson.

12

Clairvoyance and Clairaudience

The reunion was reaching its final phase. Two well-filled hours had passed rapidly. Raul Silva looked at his watch and announced to the companions that it was time for the final prayers of gratitude. These will bring aid to our suffering friends and restore the worker's energy.

A small pitcher of fresh water was placed on the table. Hilario asked if we would be attending a special ceremony and the mentor explained affably:

"No, nothing of the kind. The container of water will receive high quality magnetic resources to achieve the psychophysical equilibrium for those present."

We had barely heard this when Clementino approached the pitcher and, thoughts completely elevated in prayer, he appeared to us to be immersed in light. He extended his hands over the container and radiant particles of light were projected over and completely absorbed by the crystalline liquid.

"Magnetized water," continued Aulus, "provides a priceless therapy. There are lesions and deficiencies in the spiritual body that are reflected in the corporeal body. For now, they can only be alleviated through the magnetic intervention, until such time when the interested party can initiate his own cure."

Silva asked the mediums to be ready to receive, by way of sight or hearing, the teachings of the spiritual friends of the institution. We observed that Celina, Eugenia and Castro became more attentive.

After completing the magnetization of the water, he showed a great care for them when applying "passes"[10] to the frontal region.

---

[10]**N.T.: PASSES:** ("pass," laying on of hands). The donation of spiritual energies or vital fluids from a medium and/or spiritic source to a patient. Spiritist divides *passes* into three types: (1) magnetic, in which the energy source is the medium; (2) spiritual, in which the energy source is the spirit; and (3) mixed, in which the source is both. Spiritists believe that, in practice, most *passes* are of the third type. (David J. Hess – *"Spirits and Scientists – Ideology, Spiritism and Brazilian Culture"* 1991 The Pennsylvania State University)Webster's New Collegiate Dictionary – Pass: "A moving of the hands over or along something. "Merriam-Webster's Collegiate Dictionary – Pass: to serve as a medium of exchange

"Our friend," explained the mentor "is assisting the mediums to improve their sensorial field. They should not attempt open their clairvoyance or clairaudience just now. In the sphere of reincarnated Spirits, we maintain order by controlling perceptions. Each one of us should serve doing our best.

"Let us imagine a radio that can pick-up, simultaneously, the entire longitude of the wavelength. The transmission would be null and void, and there would not be a constructive purpose in the message. Similarly, the mediums should never preoccupy themselves by responding to all the questions with which they are bombarded. This would be a risk to the balance of influences of the ambient, unless, due to their own evolvement, they could manage these influences. Therefore, they could take on the task of selecting, among these many questions those that are towards goodness and could be used to teach the people around them."

Hilario pondered for a moment, and asked: "Is this mediumship task equally rigorous for the three mediums?"

"No, not at all. There are different mediumistic expressions and, therefore, the degree of perception varies in each one of us. Each Spirit has. Each Spirit lives developed its own mental and spiritual ability. There are variations in the mediumistic work from individual to individual just as the interpretations of life differ from soul to soul.

"Even when mediumistic faculties are identical, each person has his or her own particular manner of using them. A group of artists may work from the same model, yet each of them projects his or her personal sensitivity and style on the canvas. A lamp can emit a luminous clarity but light's appearance changes when filtered. Although it continues to burn with the same intensity, its potential is reduced as it takes on the characteristics of the filter.

"Mediumship is characterized by affinity and filtrationamong the forces with which it harmonizes, and transmits them according to the concepts that characterize its being."

Cognizant of the care that brother Clementino employed in preparing the mediums, my colleague inquired:

"Is the ability of clairvoyance and clairaudience found in the eyes and in the ears of the reincarnated individual?"

Aulus caressed Hilario's head and explained:

"Hilario, it is obvious that you are just starting your journey to higher awareness. Material eyes and ears, for vision and audition, are simple apparatus, as the eyeglasses are for the eyes, and hearing aids for the ears. All perception is mental. The deaf and the blind, when properly educated, are able to hear and see with resources that are different from those commonly used. Hertz and X-rays show that there is sound and light much farther away than the limited vibratory frontiers in which they act. The medium is gifted with special neural-psychic abilities that amplify his senses."

My companion made a gesture as one who had benefited from the lesson, but respectfully expressed an objection:

"Is Celina observing and listening to brother Clementino exclusively through her physical senses?"

"Yes, but this occurs due to rooted customs. Celina believes she hears the supervisor via the auditory channels, and sees him as if her eyes were photographic equipment that functioned with her memory. These impressions are the result of habit.

"Even in the field of common impressions, although the person employs the ears and the eyes, he or she hears and sees with the brain. Further, in spite of the brain using the cells of the cortex to select the sounds and engrave the images, it is the mind that, in reality, can see and hear. All physiological senses belong to the soul, which is really what anchors them in the physical body according to the established principles for the evolvement of the reincarnated Spirits on Earth."

And smiling, he added:

"You possess proof of this from the 'out-of-body' experiences, which occur every night while dreaming. Listening and observing take place, in spite of the physical organs' inactivity, during the experience denoted as *life of dreams*."

Then, lowering his tone of voice, he added:

"We are receptors of a greatly reduced capacity facing the innumerable forms of energy that reach us from all of the domains of the universe, receiving solely a humble gamma of these rays. In essence, our mind is a limited spiritual point, which is developed in knowledge and love, in the infinite and glorious spirituality of God.

A few moments passed.

"Let us concentrate our attention in prayer, learning the service of goodness."

Clementino spoke this phrase in a clear, slow voice offering a point on which our thoughts could converge. Attentive to our study, however, I observed the mediums more directly involved in this task.

Celina distinguished his words with precision and maintained an attitude of a disciplined student. Eugenia assimilated them as if she were receiving intuitive instructions, showing herself to be a strict apprentice. Castro, on the other hand, did not perceive anything.

With the supervisor's permission, we began our analysis. The three mediums were subtly tied to Clementino's fluidic energy, and each of them in his or her own way, acknowledged his presence.

Celina registered his most subtle movements, similar to a student facing a professor. Eugenia noted his proximity with less ease, as if she were distinguishing him through a nebulous sheet. Castro, although observing him clearly, appeared to be unaware of the instructor's influence.

"Celina's and Castro's clairvoyant and clairaudient abilities are more prominent than our sister Eugenia's," clarified Aulus with kindness.

"The three are lightly controlled by Clementino's magnetic commands and recognize his presence with their respective observations. This is because under the circumstances in which they are operating, they act using their normal senses."

"Meanwhile," Hilario questioned, "if the trio has been placed under the magnetic direction of the supervisor, why is it that our sisters accepted his invitation, while Castro is still visibly impervious to his influence?"

"The mentor of the Center exerts a gentle influence, avoiding any strong pressure that could provoke a vicious reaction unfavorable to our friends," said Aulus with conviction.

"On the other hand, we note that Castro is unable to concentrate on the higher task, interested instead in having an encounter with his discarnate mother. He considers the mentor as someone whom he is required to deal with in passing, but he has no desire to listen to him or serve him because of family issues. Therefore, he hears nothing of that which at this time interests the collective effort of the reunion."

Evidently wanting to cast a light on the lesson using our terrestrial knowledge, he added:

"He is as an antenna that suddenly became insensitive, and so cannot receive the wavelength seeking it."

At that moment we perceived a likeable companion of our plane coming from the circle of spectators toward Celina and calling to her discreetly. The noble sister heard his voice, but did not go back. She responded to him, however, by thought, and the phrase she said was clearly audible to us: "We will meet later."

Aulus immediately informed us:

"It is our sister's affectionate discarnate husband who comes to visit her. Celina is disciplined, though, and knows how to put aside any consolation she might take in hearing from him. She is intent upon collaborating in the success of the task at hand, and not interrupting its important orderliness."

Later, we saw Castro once again out of his body, motivated by a strong desire to remove himself from the circle. Dressed by the effluvia that disfigured his perispirit, he walked instantly toward the friendly entity that awaited him a short distance away.

"Our cooperator," said the mentor, "is not

accustomed to constructive discipline and considers that he has completed his personal assistance to the work program for the night. He leaves to look for his dear mother, who is being assisted by our group."

The time for questions was over. Clementino, at the head of the assembly, raised his arms and assumed a position of prayer. A light of splendorous sapphire now emanated from his chest, giving the impression that he had been converted into a wingless angel. Soon afterward, a luminous ray descended from on high, crowning his forehead. His hands radiated a prodigious magnetic force of light that reached all of us, incarnates and discarnates, lavishing us with a sensation of indescribable well-being.

Although questions ran through my mind, I was not able to speak. In our silence, the beatitude of the mentor overcame us. Those few minutes of wordless vibrations represented a beautiful waterfall of restorative energy for whoever opened the compartments of the spirit. I was able to perceive this owing to the new strength of my own energy.

Completing this unforgettable operation, Raul asked them to wait for a few additional moments and maintain their inner peace. It was up to the group to wait for the manifestation of some of the guides of the Center to close the reunion with an exposition of general instructions.

Celina asked permission to announce that she had seen a crystal stream in whose waters many of the patients were bathing. Eugenia said that she had perceived a building filled with children who were singing hymns of praises to God.

We were surprised when we heard these revelations. We could not recall anything to make us think of a current of healing waters, nor any pavilion for the protection of infants. In addition, the living room was too narrow to display such scenes.

Looking at me intrigued, Hilario asked if the two mediums could be under the influence of a momentary negative disturbance. Responding to our surprise the mentor replied:

"Each of them is united to Clementino's magnetic vibrations and picks up the images that his mind suggests to them. They viewed his thoughts to assist the sick and to form a school for our brothers and sisters, which they intend to establish soon.

"Forcefully, elaborated ideas generate forms, movement, sound and color, perfectly perceptible by all those synchronized with the wavelength that expresses them. Some phenomena of clairvoyance and clairaudience arise from the active observation of the mediums. They can identify persons, places and other things outside themselves, similarly to the common terrestrial perceptions. On the other hand, there are others that come from the suggestions brought to the medium by the creative thoughts of discarnate and incarnate friends. All of these stimulus are translated by the mind of each medium according to his or her personal abilities, favoring the most diverse interpretations."

"Oh!" exclaimed Hilario enthusiastically. "These are the same techniques as those used by obsessing Spirits on their victims, when they inflict upon them the most varied hallucinatory impressions."

"Yes," confirmed the mentor. "Exactly. Let us stop our conversation, however, as the meeting is about to conclude."

13

Thought and Mediumship

A profound and respectful silence came over the group as we awaited the closing message. The ambient was more pleasant and less grave than before.

A brilliant beam of light appeared over Celina's head. From that moment on she was ecstatic, completely separated from her physical body and surrounded by bluish radiations. Admiring this beautiful phenomenon, I faced the mentor with a questioning look. He quickly explained.

"Our sister Celina will be transmitting the words of a benefactor far from here, who will communicate with us through teledynamic energy, which unites him with the mind of the medium."

"Is this possible?" – questioned Hilario discreetly.

Aulus answered immediately:

"Consider radio and television: an individual can hear the message of a companion in a different city and see him as well if both of them are well synchronized by the same longitudinal wavelength. Celina is familiar with the sublime forces that envelop her and she yields to them confidently, assimilating the mental current of energy that seeks her. She radiates the lesson automatically, just as occurs in an unconscious trance communication, because the spiritual friend finds her cerebral cells and nervous energy as piano keys in a well tuned, harmonious and accommodating piano."

The mentor suddenly went mute, fixating his eyes on the potent floodlight of sapphire that formed and extended to every corner of the room. I contemplated the surroundings. The medium's face reflected a mysterious well-being unknown on Earth. The happiness that possessed her appeared to be contagious to all present.

I wanted to continue observing her but the mentor's right hand touched me lightly, eliciting my attention and respect. Celina's voice was relaying in clear and moving tone:

"Dear friends," started the instructor that aided us from a great distance, "let us guard the peace that Jesus bequeathed to us in order to serve Him in peace.

"With regard to mediumship, let us not overlook the important role that thought plays. Our soul lives where the heart is. We proceed influenced by our own creations, wherever we may be.

"Gravity in the mental field is as effective as in the field of physical experience. By serving the general progress, the soul moves about in the glory of goodness. By enclosing itself in selfishness, it drags in lack of equilibrium through the shadows of evil.

"Divine law seeks the good of all. To collaborate in the execution of its wise purposes is to illuminate the mind and to clarify life. To stand in its way with the pretext of favoring pernicious whims is to darken reasoning and to coagulate the shadows around our own self.

"It is indispensable to judge carefully our own steps to avoid the fog of disturbances and the painful anguish of remorse. In the domain of the spirit, neutrality does not exist.

"We evolve with the eternal light according to God's designs or we become stagnant in the shadows according to the erroneous determination of our very own *self*.

"It is not enough just to incarnate or discarnate. The making and unmaking of forms is a commonplace occurrence. What is important is the inner renovation to enhance our vision in order to move forward within the genuine notion of eternity.

"A charged conscience with malignant goals, dressed with remorse, full of disorderly ambitions or darkened with afflictions, can only attract similar forces that chain them to infernal whirlwinds. Obsession is the result of the sinister union of the mind along with the personal imbalance of darkness.

"We think and give life to the object idealized. The visible expression of our most intimate thoughts denounces our spiritual condition, and those who have affinity with the nature of our inclinations and desires approach us through what our thoughts say.

"If we persist in the lowest sphere of the human experience, those who comply with this work are attracted to us by our inferior impulses, absorbing the mental substances that we emit and projecting over us their dysfunctional elements.

"To imagine is to create; and all creation has life and movement, which, although brief, imposes responsibility to the conscience that manifests it. And since life and movement perpetuate the principles that direct relations, it is vital that we analyze what we give in order to know what it is that we are to receive.

"As for one who only thinks of anguish and crime, misery and disturbances, could one reflect in the mirror of one's own soul other images than that of disharmony and suffering? Depraved individuals, living among saints, could not evaluate their purity, since they feed on their own vibrations, and could not discern further than their own darkness.

"Those who live searching for rocks in the street surely would not find only small and insignificant pebbles. Those who delay indefinitely in measuring mud have the propensity to drown in the mire. The traveler who is fascinated by the briers that border the road runs the risk of losing his or her mind among the thorns of the savage forest.

"Let us pay attention to our thoughts, purifying them with the incessant practice of righteousness, in order to dislodge ourselves from the shackles that chain us to the dark processes of the inferior life.

"It is in the very place of the idea that the wings of the angels and the chains of the condemned are forged.

"Through our thoughts we enslave ourselves to the branches of the infernal suffering, sentencing us at times to centuries of pilgrimage over the paths of pain and death.

"Tortured mediumship is nothing more than the union of souls compromised in afflictive trials in order to clear up prior debts. Incarnate or discarnate, whatever the degree of expiation, it is indispensable to renew ourselves. This is the only means of recuperating harmony and shortening the torments that plague in a thousand ways.

"The individual who is satisfied solely with religious expertise without making any effort toward one's inner improvement, can be compared with the person who accepts an honored title among people and rejects the responsibility that it imposes. It is very dangerous for the soul.

"Titles of faith do not constitute mere words with which we can cover our deficiencies and weaknesses. They express obligations of purification from which we will not be permitted to escape without renouncing the obligations they impart.

"In our work circle, therefore, it will not be enough to believe and to convince. No one can be called a Spiritist simply for being cured of a persistent illness with the aid of friendly entities and, convinced by this, admits the intervention of the spiritual world in his or her existence. Also, no one is a medium, in the elevated sense, solely because one is the instrument for communication between visible and invisible beings.

"To adapt ourselves to the superior principles that illuminate our path, it is necessary to instill their essence into our life as a testimony of our conversion to sanctifying love. It is not enough, therefore, merely to meditate about our superior idealism. It is imperative to live it in our daily existence.

"Great artists know how to place the spark of

genius in a simple brush stroke, a small block of marble, or a simple musical composition. Souls truly converted to Christ reflect His beauty in the briefest gestures of each hour, be it in the spark of a short phrase, in the secret aid given to the neighbors, or in the silent renunciation unknown by the others.

"Our thoughts generate our actions and our actions engender the thoughts of others. Let us inspire sympathy and evolvement, nobility and kindness around us, so that we will not lack the precious bread of happiness tomorrow.

"To be certain that we are immortal without improving our spirit is as to illuminate a barren place. To mediate between spiritual world and Earth without lifting our morals is to stagnate in sterility. Thought is as significant in mediumship as the importance of the bed is for the river. Pure waters that run over a bed of mud are transformed into an adulterated current.

"It is certain that divine messages descend from heaven to Earth. For this to occur, however, it is imperative for adequate channels to exist. Jesus is waiting for human messengers capable of projecting the marvels of the Kingdom in the world.

"To reach that stage of ideal perfection, the possessors of psychic faculties must not simply receive communications. It is imperative that they concentrate all their energies in an elevated way of life, seeking the material with which to construct their own path in their own education and in altruistic service to humanity. "The communion with the guides for the spiritual progress of the world through their written words enriches our knowledge and accentuates our mental value; and the consistent planting of kindness brings the fruit of sympathy, without which the granary of existence is reduced to a cavern of desperation and discouragement.

"It is not enough to see, to hear or to be a trance medium for the discarnate Spirits to acquire respectability. In every community throughout the world, many are ignorant and irresponsible as a result of the deficient degree of evolvement. Many times, without the intentional desire for evil, millions of discarnate souls practice vampirism on the incautious incarnates, simply to continue enjoying the sensations of the physical field, which they have not desired to get rid of." To succeed, every task requires workers who are dedicated to their own growth and moral elevation. Nature shows this to us. The newborn tree bears no fruit. Wood, prior to treatment, cannot be useful at home. Shifting sands cannot guarantee firmness. A lamp that lacks oil cannot project light. The automobile cannot run smoothly where the road maker's hammer has not yet constructed a secure path.

"How can we expect to receive divine thought where human thought is spent on the lower reflections of life? What messenger of Heaven will cause the celestial message to brighten our understanding, when the mirror of our soul has darkened from the most inferior interests? Could a star be reflected in the mire of mud?

"Friends, let us put our thoughts in goodness and demonstrate it.

"Everything that exists within nature is an idea revealed outwardly. The universe is the projection of the divine mind. The political and social context of Earth is the product of the human mind.

"Civilizations and their inhabitants, cultures and experiences constitute forms of thought through which we evolve incessantly toward the higher spheres. Let us be preoccupied then with perfecting ourselves.

"Without comprehension and kindness, we will become united with the wretched and the rebel. Without studying and observing, we will be counted indefinitely among the unfortunate proponents of ignorance.

"Love and wisdom are the wings which will surely bring us to perfect communion with our celestial Father. Let us scale the superior plane instilling sublime thoughts in those souls that surround us.

"The word enlightens but it is the example that pushes us forward. Let us adapt ourselves to the redeeming Gospel. Jesus Christ is the goal of our renovation. By regenerating our existences according to His teachings we will restructure the intimate life of those souls that surround us.

"My friends, believe! A pure thought in action is a force that will compel us away from hatred into love, from pain to happiness, from Earth to heaven.

"Let us procure the conscience of Jesus so that our own conscience reflects His perfection and beauty. Let us learn to reflect His glory and love so that the celestial light manifests itself in our souls, just as the solar splendor extends over the entire world. Let us commence our personal effort of spiritual evolvement today, and tomorrow we shall have advanced considerably on the great path!

"My friends, my brothers, by praying to Jesus for the protection for all, I leave you now until we meet again soon."

The medium's voice became mute. Very moved, we all observed that up high the brilliant beam of light went out. Raul Silva closed the meeting with a brief prayer. We gathered around Clementino the moment we were ready to say our good-byes.

"Come back when you wish," he invited us graciously.

"Yes, we wish to continue learning."

And together with the mentor, we retired contentedly as if we had sipped the living water of peace from the cup of happiness.

14

In Spiritual Service

We were heading away from the Institution when Celina's discarnate husband, whose presence we had recognized during the meeting, approached us. He seemed to know our mentor because he stopped at our side and exclaimed:

"Dear mentor, please."

Aulus introduced us to the new friend.

"This is our brother Abelardo Martins. He was Celina's husband and is working to adapt himself to the work of our organization."

We could see that Abelardo was not a most cultivated Spirit. His mannerisms and voice revealed a spiritual state that was attached to earthly matters.

"My dear mentor," he continued excitedly, "I am here to ask you for your assistance with Liborio. The group's rescue assistance improved his dispositions; however, now it is the woman who pursues him."

"I see," said the mentor with goodwill, "but for this we require Celina's assistance."

And, patting him on his shoulder, he said:

"Return now to Celina. Later, when she falls asleep and separates from her physical body, return with her, so that we can be together for a little while. We will wait for you in the park close by."

Abelardo departed happily. We entered an enormous plaza populated by many trees and waited for our companions. Taking advantage of a few minutes, Aulus commented on the petition he had received:

"Abelardo is interested in Liborio, who was the first to communicate and be assisted tonight through Eugenia's intervention."

Aulus informed us that Celina's husband had wandered in desperation for a long time.

"During his life on Earth he was temperamental and could not immediately resign to the imperatives of death. He was angry and obstinate, thus shortening his lifetime due to the excesses that deteriorated his organic strength. He tried in vain to obsess his wife, to reclaim her as if she were simply a servant. Recognizing his inability to do this, he stayed for a few years in dark shadows among rebellious and disrespectful Spirits. Finally, prayers from his companion, who was assisted by many friends, succeeded in dissuading him, thereby changing his attitude.

"He gave in when he recognized the impropriety of the mental intemperance in which he found pleasure. Later, after being prepared by the group of friends whom we have just left, Abelardo was admitted into an organization in which he served as caretaker of mentally unbalanced souls."

As soon as the mentor completed this brief biography, Hilario pondered:

"Abelardo's case creates interesting questions. For instance: will he continue to be united to his wife?"

"Yes." answered the mentor. "The love between them has deep roots from the past."

"In spite of their differences?"

"Why not? Does the celestial Father fail to love us in spite of our faults?"

"Truly," my colleague declared, slightly disappointed. "None could argue that. But has Abelardo reunited with his wife?"

"Yes. He found in her a valuable incentive to commit to his self-recuperation."

"But as a discarnate Spirit, does he share a home with her?"

"As much as it is possible for him. He is far from being elevated due to his lack of discipline and confusion, and he still suffers the disagreeable consequences of the imbalances he went through. His home and his wife's tenderness are the greatest paradise that he can merit at this time.

"He dedicates himself daily to the arduous service of assisting demented companions, but rests whenever possible close to his wife. Once a week he accompanies her in reading the Gospel at home. He is her constant collaborator in mediumistic tasks. Every evening, when they feel that circumstances are favorable, both dedicate themselves to assisting the sick.

"They are not only husband and wife united by physical ties; they are dear friends. Abelardo now uses his time to clear up old debts and dreams of welcoming his wife, after having acquired additional degrees of evolvement, when Celina once again reenters the spiritual world."

"Is this common? Is the separation in marriages only imaginary?"

"One case does not establish a rule," Aulus responded good-humoredly. "Wherever affinity does not exist, the terrestrial marriage is redemption and nothing more. In the majority of unions, death of the physical body ratifies a separation that already existed in life. In those cases, the partner that discarnates retires from his trial, as would a debtor, who finds peace after having fulfilled his debts.

"Nevertheless, when the ties that unite the souls survive the emotions of a human journey, even after a second marriage, the spiritual communion continues sublimely with a constant interchange of sweet vibrations and thoughts."

Hilario reflected for a few minutes and conjectured:

"It is true. The crossing from the tomb significantly modifies the Spirit. Each traveler on his path, each heart with its own problem."

"Blessed be those who are renewed in righteousness!" exclaimed Aulus with satisfaction. "True love is progress through renunciation. Whoever does not know how to renounce in favor of the happiness of a loved one can love with enthusiasm and warmth, but will not be crowned with the glory of pure love.

"After death we usually learn, through the sacrifice of our dreams, the science of love, not according to our desires but rather in conformity with God's law: mothers who were obliged to give up their children to the trials that they need to undergo; fathers who are compelled to change their projects to protect their family; wives who are forced to yield their husbands to other female souls; husbands who are forced to accept their wives remarrying and living in the same home that they lived in. All of this we encounter on Earth. Death is a call for fraternal understanding. When we do not accept such a challenge, suffering is the ineludible consequence."

And with a great smile he added:

"When we do not know how to divide love, happiness is not able to multiple itself."

The conversation continued, interesting and animated, as Celina and Abelardo approached us. They appeared comforted and happy. Accompanied by his wife, our new friend appeared happier and radiant, as if he had absorbed vitality and enthusiasm. I noticed from Hilario's facial expressions that he had a new world of questions to ask. Notwithstanding, Aulus advised:

"Let us proceed. It is necessary to act quickly."

A short time later we entered a nebulous region within the dark night. The stars disappeared before our eyes. I had the impression of a preponderance of bituminous gas in the atmosphere.

We heard crying and cursing around us, but the small lamp that Abelardo carried permitted us to observe only the narrow road through which we were to travel. After a few minutes of marching, we reached a poorly lit construction in which various patients took refuge, assisted by attentive male nurses.

We entered. Aulus explained that we were in an emergency hospital, one of many that may be found in purgatorial regions. Poverty, need and suffering were reflected in everything.

"This is my work temple" – said Abelardo proud of being an important part of the service of assistance.

Brother Justino, the director of the institution, came toward us and greeted us. He begged forgiveness for not being able to accompany us. The institution was full of psychopathic discarnates that needed his personal assistance. However, he gave us permission to go about freely.

The disharmony in the place was so great that I could not hide my astonishment. How could we even think we could make any improvement in such a tormented atmosphere? The mentor, nonetheless, tried to clarify matters saying:

"This is a place of short-term refuge for the desperate. According to their reaction, we quickly conduct them to establishments of positive recuperation, or they return to the areas of affliction from where they came."

We reached the simple bed where Liborio lay. His absent and glassy eyes revealed a lack of interest in our presence. His appearance was that of a person crazed under the influence of occult scourging. One of the guards came toward us and said to Abelard that the hospitalized patient was in anguish. Aulus rechecked him in a fatherly manner and immediately advised:

"The constant thought of the incarnate sister that our friend is spiritually attached to is tormenting him. They are both attuned to the same wavelength. It is a case of reciprocal persecution. The benefits that he previously received in the group are now jeopardized by the suggestions that she makes from afar."

"We, therefore, have in this case," I alleged, "an exact similarity to that which we commonly refer to on Earth as tortured mediumship. They are mediums who are no longer taunted by inferior entities, yet immediately reunite with them, in spite of our great efforts to liberate them."

"Yes," agreed the mentor. "As long as they do not modify their spiritual disposition and establish new noble habits of thought, they will find themselves succumbing to a mutual enslavement, in which the obsessor and the obsessed nurture one another with reciprocal energies. They fear separation because they have an habitual affinity to one another. This impedes the double recuperation that we wish for them."

The patient was pale and in great anguish. He appeared to be going through an interior, uncontrollable and fearful storm. Everything indicated the proximity of the sister who had taken control of his mind. Our friend appeared to be more dominated and sickly.

The mentor had not even finished formulating his diagnosis when sleep caused the poor woman to disassociate from her physical body. She appeared before us, ferociously saying:

"Liborio! Liborio! Why did you leave me? Do not abandon me. Return to our home. Listen to me. Hear me!"

"What is this?" exclaimed Hilario intrigued. "Isn't this the same person who we tried to isolate from evil influences earlier tonight?"

Since the mentor responded in the affirmative, my colleague continued:

"Merciful God! Isn't she interested in restoring her own health? Didn't she ask for assistance from the institution she attends?"

"This is what she thinks she wants," explained Aulus diligently. "However, she feeds on the sick fluids of her discarnate companion and instinctively gets close to him. Thousands of others are like her. They suffer infirmities of various types and conveniently adapt to them. They make no effort to improve and consider themselves to be unfortunate and suffering. In spite of that, when these vibrations are removed, they seem to feel empty and strange, creating symptoms and impressions that attract the illnesses which manifest themselves once again. Thus, they happily remain victims."

"This occurs in the majority of obsession cases. Incarnates and discarnates unite, compelled by a strong mutual fascination, until they renew their mental inclinations. That is the reason why on many occasions the greater pains act upon minor pains and awaken the depraved souls involved in this type of inferior exchange."

At this moment she was able to get closer to Liborio and he smiled, as would a happy child. Upon recognizing the presence of Celina, the poor girl screamed angrily.

"Who is that woman? Who is she?"

Celina came close and implored humbly:

"Dear sister, calm yourself. Liborio is exhausted and sick. Let us all help him to get some rest."

The woman could not stand Celina's pleasant manner and, though she asked for the group's help, would not recognize the medium. Blinded by her jealousy, she screamed harsh words to the patient that we will not repeat, and dashed out of the room.

Liborio appeared annoyed until Aulus applied passes and restored his serenity. Immediately, the mentor told us affectionately:

"Divine grace is so great that even undignified sentiments are used for our own good. The visitor left because Celina's proximity to Liborio made her indignant and aloof. This reprieve, however, will allow us time to aid him with some necessary reflections.

"Upon awakening in her physical body, our poor friend will vaguely remember having dreamed of Liborio together with a companion, and paint from this a scene with her own impressions, for each mind perceives in others that which it feels within it."

Abelardo was satisfied. He caressed the patient, foreseeing his improvement. Hilario expressed with admiration:

"What amazes me is the incessant service everywhere. While awake and during sleep, in life as well as in death."

Aulus responded with a smile.

"Yes, inertia is simply an illusion, and laziness is a flight that the law punishes by keeping us behind."

Our task was completed and it was time to depart. Upon saying our goodbyes, Aulus promised to meet us on the following night to continue with our observations.

15
Vicious Forces

It was almost nightfall. The day had been warm and people filed down the public highway, anxiously seeking fresh air. We were headed towards another Spiritist Center with Aulus, who was continuing our work program, when loud shouting attracted our attention.

Two policemen were escorting an older man away from a modest restaurant. He was deplorably drunk, kicking and shouting harsh words, and protesting continuously.

"Observe our poor brother," said the mentor.

Since he had just entered the police car, we stopped to observe. A dark shadow-like Spirit, something akin to a strange octopus, embraced him. Drink had taken over both of them. Juxtaposed, they appeared to have the same disturbances. The driver of the vehicle blew his horn and left hurriedly. The scene offered a valuable lesson.

Noting Hilario's expression, the mentor considered that we had enough time to reach some interesting conclusions, and he invited us to enter the restaurant. The place was crowded with many happy people. Surely we would be able to obtain material here for some particular lesson. We went inside.

The ambient produced an indefinable feeling of discomfort. Near habitual smokers and drinkers were sad discarnate Spirits in a state of expectancy. Some absorbed mouthfuls of smoke, which were exhaled into the air still warm from the lungs that expulsed it, finding happiness and nourishment in this. Others breathed in vapors of the impenitent alcoholics. Pointing to them, the mentor informed us:

"Many of our brothers, who have already separated from their physical body, attach themselves with such delirium to physical sensations that it leads them to co-exist with our terrestrial friends, temporarily unbalanced by the disagreeable habits that dominate them."

"But why do they yield to pleasures of this kind?

"Hilario," said the mentor kindly, "what begins in life continues after death. These companions fix their minds on the lowest appetites of the world, feeding on animal-like emotions. In spite of having frequented religious sanctuaries, they were not preoccupied with the principles of the faith they embraced. Existence for them is the cult of undignified satisfactions and the exaltation of the astute and the strong.

"Death found them in a sphere of dark and depraved acts. Since the law requires that each soul receive in accordance with that which he contributed, they are interested only in places where they can nurture their illusions. For this reason, they fear the truth and abominate it, behaving like an owl that flees from the light."

Showing pity, my colleague asked:

"Meanwhile, how will they reform?"

"The day will come when nature itself will empty their glass," responded Aulus with conviction. "There are thousands of readjusting processes in the infinite universe, whereby God's will is done. Some of them we can name affliction, disenchantment, exhaustive annoyance, suffering and prison."

"In spite of all," I pondered, "these unfortunate Spirits will not tire completely of their desires soon, because they satisfy them."

"I agree," responded the mentor, "however, even if they do not tire, the Divine law will conduct them to a regenerating prison."

"How?"

Hilario asked, and the mentor quickly explained:

"There are some reincarnations that involve a painful expiatory battle for those souls attracted to vices. We have, for example, Down syndrome, paralysis, blindness, epilepsy, idiotism, birth defects and many other afflictions that, although anguishing, are necessary. They act to benefit the unbalanced mind from the cradle throughout youth. Most of the time, similar curative processes provide good results because the trials they bring about are obligatory.

"However," I asked, "what if our coarse incarnate brothers and sisters resolved to reconsider their attitudes? What if they returned to harmony by way of a mental renovation based on righteousness?"

"Ah, then they would regain time, recuperating and collaborating efficiently with discarnate friends. Using their will, they would achieve true miracles. To do so, however, they would have to make a heroic effort."

Observing the drunkards whose glasses were also enjoyed by their invisible co-participants, Hilario remembered:

"Yesterday, we studied mediumship in a temple where the suffering discarnates that needed assistance used mediums to express themselves. Here we perceive vicious entities in perfect communion with inferior forces that take advantage of people with which they are harmonious. Would it be correct to consider both as types of mediumship?"

"Without a doubt," confirmed the mentor. "All kinds of psychic resources are available to everyone, just as movement or breathing are forces that incarnate or discarnate Spirits may employ for good or evil. Mediumship is neither granted nor earned.

"We often encounter mediums who are controlled and subjugated by somber and delinquent entities with which they harmonize. This leads to scandal and confusion instead of goodness.

"For this reason, to serve requires more than mediumistic faculties. We must rely on the Spiritist doctrine and pure Christianity to control the mediumistic energy and entrust it to spiritual improvement through religious faith, just as we control electricity to benefit human comfort."

Aulus quickly glanced at some nearby reserved rooms as if he were familiar with them. Noticing a particular door, he invited us to open it. Together we followed him.

At a table well-provided with fine cognac, we found a young man smoking profusely. He wrote continuously under the control of an entity whose repellent aspect called for compassion.

"Let us study this case," suggested the mentor.

A dark pasty substance flowing from the hands of the sad brother accompanying him impregnated the young man's brain. Through these characteristics we could verify the bond between them. The couple did not notice our presence.

"At this very moment," Aulus announced attentively, "our unknown brother is an able psychograph medium. The entity completely controls his expressive thought cells. He is attached to his imagination and ideas, acceding to his occult will through magnetic induction. The young man wants to produce risqué pages and has found the one that could help him by feeding his mind."

And producing a particular expression in his voice added:

"We always find what we seek to be."

After a brief reflective pause, Hilario again commenced:

"Is he a medium? Could he be an active part of some common spiritual group?"

"No, he is not under any spiritual discipline. He is a young man with a lively intelligence but without great experience in life, and controlled by evil entities."

After he had bent over the two for a few moments, the mentor benevolently said:

"Between the excitement produced by alcohol and smoke that they both inhale and enjoy, they intend to create a scandal that is going to cause a sad family affliction. There was a homicide and it appears that a certain girl is associated with the deplorable incident.

"The young man is a friend of a well-known newspaper reporter. Being, himself a malicious person, his mental antenna is linked with the more deplorable aspects of this problem. He responded to a request to collaborate with the newspaper reporter and found an inflexible and vicious persecutor of the girl referred to. The persecuting Spirit is interested in exaggerating her participation in the occurrence, and intent on beating down her apprehensive mind and ruining her youth."

"But how?" asked Hilario frightened.

"The newspaper man intends to publish the young man's slanderous commentary. If he does, it will disturb the girl, since she did not play the part in the crime in the way they intend to relate. The obsessor, using the young man to write this story, is going to cause a public sensation in order to lead her to a moral crisis and succeed in corrupting her character. If he has his way, he could drag her to the vicious pool with him."

"Will he achieve his goal?" insisted my astonished colleague.

"Who can know?"

With sadness the mentor added:

"Of course the girl would have previously chosen the type of trials that she would have to endure and be disposed to fight valiantly against temptations."

"And if she does not have the necessary strength to combat?"

"It would be more justifiable to say, 'if she did not have the desire;' as Divine law does not present us with problems far greater than our capacity to resolve them. Therefore, if she were to decide not to combat the destructive influence, she will continue to suffer the disturbances that already affect her."

"And why is all of this necessary?"

Hilario's question arose from an afflictive interrogation; nonetheless, Aulus tranquillized us, explaining:

"Without a doubt, the young girl and the unfortunate one that pursues her have been united for a long time. Prior to this reincarnation, which has been beneficial to her, they were together in the inferior zones. As a Spirit, re-encountering her in the physical world, he is planning on unbalancing her emotional state and exploiting her through his vampirizing action."

Aulus paused briefly, and smiled adding:

"However, to speak of the matter would be to turn back to the moving pages of a grand romance that would lead us away from the objective we desire to reach. Let us restrict ourselves to mediumship."

To relieve us from Hilario's many questions, I declared:

"This situation induces us to meditate over the general phenomenon of interchange in which the entire human race revolves without perceiving it."

"Ah yes!" agreed the mentor. "The mediumistic faculties and cooperation of the spiritual world appear everywhere. Where thoughts exist, mental currents exist. Where there are mental currents, associations exist; and all associations are interdependent and influence each other. Therefore, it is necessity to live nobly to attract thoughts that enrich us.

"Dignified work, kindness, fraternal understanding, service to our fellow beings, respect for nature, and prayer constitute the purest means of assimilating the superior principles of life. Spiritually, we give and receive in the plane of the ideas according to the universal laws which we can never escape from."

With a silent gesture, which reminded us of our obligations, the mentor invited us to leave. We went into the street. As soon as we started to walk, an ambulance went by us slowly, beeping loudly, trying to make way.

Alongside the driver a man was seated, whose gray hair adorned his pleasant but worried face. Next to him, gently and sweetly caressing him, was an entity dressed in white violet, surrounding his head with soft soothing radiations of silvery light.

"Oh!" inquired Hilario with curiosity. "Who could that gentleman be so well accompanied?"

Aulus smiled and explained:

"Not everything on the common path is vicious energy. It is probably a doctor involved in a medical task."

"But, is he a spiritist?"

"With all the due respect that we owe Spiritism, it is imperative to remember that the Lord's blessings can descend over any religious expression," affirmed the mentor with an expression of tolerance. "Above all, he must be a generous and professional humanitarian who, because of his habit of aiding his brothers and sisters, merits the assistance he is receiving. It is not enough to have the title of spiritist and medical doctor to attract the beneficial influence that accompanies him. To maintain so great an affinity and harmony with the Spirit that aids him, he must possess a good conscience and a heart that radiates peace and fraternity."

"Can we categorize him as a medium?" – asked my friend a bit disconcerted.

"Of course!" – responded Aulus with conviction. "He is a medium of valuable human blessings, mainly in assisting the sick. He incorporates in his work the mental energy of the genies of goodness dedicated to love for the suffering of the Earth."

And, with an expressive inflection in his voice, added:

"As we can see, the forces of good and evil in this evolutive sphere in which we find ourselves arise in every way. We register the existence of mediumistic faculties according to the happy or unhappy, correct or undignified way in which each mind assimilates them. By studying mediumship in the spiritist sanctuaries with Jesus, we truly observe a force unique to each soul. Anyone can take advantage of this force and use it for maximum goodness if it is used with discipline.

"Let us remember that electricity, little by little, transforms the face of the world. It is not enough to possess a powerful waterfall with the potential of millions of horsepower. It is indispensable to install a dam next to it to control those resources, increasing and distributing them, according to the needs of each one. Without it, the waterfall will be a living picture of phenomenal beauty, but a lamentable waste."

Time did not allow us to prolong our conversation; we therefore proceeded toward a group where our studies of the previous evening would continue.

16

The Mediumistic Mandate

It was almost 8:00 pm when we stopped in front of a somber looking building surrounded by parked vehicles. People entered and left, and a great number of discarnates congregated both inside and out.

Some guards of our plane spread out attentively, impeding the access to impenitent and mocking Spirits. Various groups of people entered the Center but once in the lobby they were separated from certain Spirits that were following them. These Spirits were not simply curious or in pain, but rather blasphemers who are persistent in doing evil.

Nevertheless, those cases constituted an exception. The majority of the retinue of discarnate brothers and sisters was integrated with afflicted and sick people, and in as much need of fraternal assistance as the ill and anguished patients whom they were accompanying. We entered.

A large luminous cord, which acted as a partition, surrounded a big table in the center of an ample size living room. Around it, a great area was reserved, where the incarnates and discarnates needing assistance were seated. This area appeared to be equally protected by rays of magnetic defense under the care of the Spirits-guards.

On the opposite side of the entrance, several spiritual benefactors conferred. Close by, a respectable lady listened tenderly to a diverse group of patients. She had an extensive aura of opal radiations. As she conversed with the suffering people, some tried to interfere with her by projecting dark substances. The sickly fluids, however, could not reach her force field. Signaling her, the mentor informed us:

"She is our sister Ambrosina, who for over 20 years has offered what she best possesses in this existence. Through her Christian mediumship and her love of our ideals, she renounced the simplest happiness in the world. She does not have a husband, children or even a house she can call her own.

Ambrosina had gray hair and was old and wrinkled; however, a peace vibrated from her being. We saw a small cone of light similar to a delicate adornment. Intrigued, we consulted with our mentor, and he clarified:

"It is an ultra sensitive magnetic apparatus. Through it, the medium lives in constant contact with the Spirit responsible for her work. She has long been dedicated to the cause of goodness and has made many sacrifices. For this, Ambrosina received a mediumistic mandate of service from the superior plane, meriting a most intimate association with her instructor. Her influence grows through her ministry of fraternity and comprehension. Since she inspires hope and faith, she receives some of the most disconcerting requests."

"Do the requests and pleas cause her to live as a martyr?" asked Hilario, inevitably curious.

"To a great extent yes, because she bridges two worlds. She cannot solve all the problems presented to her. Because of her evangelical patience, however, she knows how to assist others so they can help themselves."

We approached the respectable and modest medium. She appeared pensive in spite of the loud disturbing voices around her. Nearby, two men reflected lamentable scenes revealing a crime in which they were involved. Observing them, Ambrosina began to speak so that only we could hear.

"Dear spiritual friends, what should I do? I know the thoughts of our delinquent brothers. A man was killed. Through the thoughts of those responsible, I feel the man's agony. What do these fugitives of the Earth's justice seek here?"

The medium did not want to think of the crime and thus loose her normal harmonious vibrations. At this point, one of the mentors present approached her and restored her tranquility saying:

"Ambrosina, be calm and do not fear. It is imperative that their affliction does not disturb us. View our unfortunate companions as creatures worthy of our pity. Bear in mind that we are here to assist and that remedies are not for the healthy. Feel compassion, but control your equilibrium. We are debtors of love who respect one another, but assistance is required for the more unfortunate. Receive our brothers as patients who are compromised by evil and desire our warmth."

The medium became serene. She then re-initiated the conversation in a more natural manner with those visiting the Center.

Someone was soliciting aid for a tormented heart, asking to assist their unfortunate disgraced relative. We heard pleads to assist sick and need people. Ambrosina consoled and promised to help. These problems would be presented to the mentor Gabriel when he arrived. Without a doubt he would offer what was needed.

A few moments later Gabriel, who was held in the highest regard in the Center, arrived. He entered the room accompanied by a great number of friends. They faced the table and chatted amicably. Spirits of the noblest mental life were logically united, creating a large beam of light, which was inaccessible to the shadows that controlled the majority of incarnates and discarnates at the meeting.

Gabriel and his companions embraced us warmly. Aulus often expressed his admiration for self-sacrificing and cultured mentors such as Gabriel. We shared a brilliant festivity with the instructors and spiritual functionaries of the Institution. Treating patients and the suffering did not lessen their hope, peace and optimism. With them were doctors, professors, nurses and auxiliary discarnates. All wanted to serve.

They radiated so much beauty and happiness that I was surprised when Hilario commenced the questioning that characterized his youthful temperament.

"Considering the radiation of light and affection they project, could they be ambassadors of the divine Providence? Could they be living among Saints? Could they be living in constant personal communion with the Christ? Are their impeccable souls?"

The mentor smiled good humouredly and explained:

"Not so. In spite of all the affection that is due to them, they are vanguards of progress but not infallible. They are great souls achieving the blessed process of purification, meriting our reverence because of the degree of evolvement that they have already accomplished. Notwithstanding, they are Spirits still attached to the Earth, where they will reincarnate, fulfilling the universal law of reincarnation and serving their development."

"In facing this assembly of tortured souls, however, are they luminaries exempt of errors?"

"No," stressed Aulus with understanding. "We cannot expect qualities from them that are only witnessed in absolutely pure Spirits. They are proponents of fraternity and superior conscience; however, they can still err. They outshine due to their goodwill, culture, and personal sacrifice to assist reincarnated companions.

"Nevertheless, they can fall victim to their errors. They quickly correct these, however, without the vanity common to learned people on Earth. Here, for instance, we have various doctors without the corporeal body. In spite of being excellent professionals, dedicated and meritorious in the mission that they have embraced, it would not be realistic that they leap from fragmentary scientific knowledge to integral wisdom. Understanding death, they acquire new visions of life as their observations expand. They realize that they know something, but it is very little in comparison with what they must still learn.

"They devote themselves to beautiful crusades of service in which they not only assist but learn. Workers from other circles of human experiences also find themselves in a similar situation. They aid and are aided; it could not be otherwise. We know that miracles do not exist, as they would represent a derogation of the law of nature. We are brothers and sisters, evolving jointly in a process of interdependence in which achievement relieves individual effort."

As we received Aulus' words with jubilance, Ambrosina sat by the side of the director of the meeting. He was an agreeable looking gray haired man who displayed simplicity and faith. He was in charge of organizing the orientation of the fourteen people at the worktable.

While Gabriel applied longitudinal passes to the medium to prepare her for the evening's forthcoming activities, the conductor of the reunion said a heartfelt prayer. An edifying text of the doctrinaire teachings was then read, followed by a brief evangelical message. In the latter selection, Gabriel's influence over the director of the Center prevailed.

Patience was the main theme of the reading. This was especially helpful because the assembly appeared affected by disquieting problems. Patience would restore the group's equilibrium.

Dozens of people grouped around the table exhibiting their trials and tribulations. Strange thought-forms emerged from each group, manifesting each personal mental condition. We perceived darts of preoccupation and bitterness and a heavy fog of tears. Obsessors controlled by disappointment and desperation expressed vengeance, obviously worsened by the fear of the unknown.

A great number of discarnates longed for heaven while others, disoriented by the false religious education received on Earth, feared hell. Various spiritual friends inspired those seated at the director's worktable through the doctrinaire teaching based on the evangelical theme of the evening. In this way, the unfortunates heard good comments that both motivated and consoled.

Individual failings were not revealed and although we could clearly perceive that the advice was anonymous, it had precise directness. These friends brought joy to hearts battered with disenchantment, a warning to negligent consciences, and a feeling of renewed forgiveness, faith, charity and hope. Also present were impressive scenes of Spirits trying to hypnotize their victims during a sleep they provoked, preventing them from paying attention to the constructive messages.

Many mediums worked in the room, collaborating harmoniously in general service. Nevertheless, we observed that Ambrosina was the center of everyone's confidence and attention. In her giving and receiving she was the heart of the Sanctuary, the living center of the silent connection between the inhabitants of the two distinct spheres.

Numerous sheets of paper were placed next to her as she held herself in deep prayer. They were anxious petitions, desires and supplications from the people who sought the protection of the Heavens for their afflictions. Each sheet was an emotional petition, a moving plea.

Between Ambrosina and Gabriel one could now perceive an extensive elastic band of bluish light over which the spiritual friends entered one by one holding the arm of the medium, desiring Christian solidarity. After influencing her cortical centers as much as possible, the spiritual counselors attended the problems expressed.

Prior to responding to the questions, however, the spiritual workers of the institution placed a great fluidic mirror close to the medium. In it, with incredible rapidity, there appeared the images of the people mentioned in the evening's petition. The intent was to submit these for the examination of the benefactors, who would contemplate their image at a distance, pick up their thoughts and specify what each needed. Afterward, a possible solution pertaining to the requested solicitations was offered.

While knowledgeable companions of faith demonstrated the path of inner peace inspired by the mentors from our plane, Ambrosina, under the direction of instructors who alternated in the service of assistance, psychographed endlessly.

The work in the room slowed, signaling that we could now ask questions. Hilario was the first to ask about something that we could not interpret. Referring to the enormous fluidic tie that linked Ambrosina to her mentor, he asked:

"What is the purpose of that band which intimately connects the medium and her protector?"

Aulus, with his usual tolerance and benevolence, responded:

"The greater development of the mediumistic faculties requires this. Listening to and observing the vibrations that transcend the common sensorial field, Ambrosina cannot be at the mercy of all the requests from the spiritual plane. She would risk the loss of her equilibrium.

"When the mediums' goodwill, studies and comprehension of their responsibilities increase, they affirm their service to righteousness, and receive greater and more constant assistance. Wise and experienced spiritual friends will guide their tasks on Earth and control their strength. Gabriel, for example, is the perfect administrator of the energies of our sister, who establishes contact with the spiritual plane solely under his supervision."

"Does this mean that to establish a communication for study purposes using this lady as our intermediary, we must tune in to her and her mentor at the same time?"

"Exactly," replied Aulus visibly satisfied, "a mediumistic mandate demands order, security and efficiency. To delegate authority is to concede power and resources from anyone who authorizes it. It is not proper to seek indiscriminate cooperation from the medium without offering the necessary guarantees."

"Does not this impede the transmission of the communications?"– asked Hilario.

"In no way. Presented with a respectable and logical request, Gabriel's mission is to facilitate communication in the same manner that he aids the medium."

I inquired if a perfect communion between the mentor and protégée indicated an obligation assumed by the mediums prior to reincarnation. Aulus responded solicitously:

"Oh yes, such services do not occur without prior programming. Chance is a word used to explain that of which mankind is not aware. Gabriel and Ambrosina planned this precise experience prior to her return to the physical life."

Remembering the words of the mentor I asked: "Why do you say that when the mediums affirm their service to righteousness, they receive the firm and constant assistance of spiritual friends, since they are already united?"

The mentor looked directly at me and said:

"We must bear in mind free-will. Ambrosina made an agreement to serve. She can cancel this, however, in spite of our recognizing her excellence and magnitude. She could decide to employ a new route to her idealism as a woman, although this would delay her ability to break her ties to the world.

"The mentors of the spiritual world seek companions, not slaves. The medium that is worthy of the mission of assistance is not a chained animal, but rather a humane brother or sister who aspires to wisdom. He or she should work and study out of love.

"It is for this reason that many commence the journey and then retreat. Free to decide their own destiny, often they prefer to remain in undesirable company and fall into terrible fascinations. Initially, they are enthusiastic to server, but then begin to listen to corrupt elements due to their lack of vigilance.

"They trip and fall into lust, indolence, personal destruction, or into sensual delinquency that transform them into toys of the adversaries of the Light. These adversaries vampirize their strength and annihilate their greatest possibilities. This has always occurred."

"Yes, yes," I admitted, "but wouldn't it be possible for the spiritual mentors to take precautionary measures and interrupt the abuses as they appear?"

The mentor smiled and humbly responded:

"Each conscience marches by itself, in spite of the numerous teachers on the path. We cause our own defeat or victory. Individually and collectively, we acquire experiences to redeem or evolve through our efforts. Human beings construct, destroy, and reconstruct destinies, as humankind creates and eliminates civilizations, seeking the best direction in response to God's call.

"It is for this reason that heavy tribulations martiryze the world. Illnesses and afflictions, wars and miseries are heavy tribulations, yet awaken just discernment in each soul. Each person lives in the sphere of one's personal conquests or one's personal debts. We see, on the planet millions of beings under a tortured mediumship and thousands possessing brilliant psychic faculties, many of whom force themselves to develop these same resources.

"Very few obtain a mediumistic mandate for fraternal solidarity and light. To exercise a sublime mediumship is a service to which we should all strive, even though this glorious acquisition costs us many centuries."

"But would it be possible for Ambrosina, who exercises a mediumistic mandate, to fall into error?"

"Of course," stressed the mentor. "A mandate is a proxy of the permission obtained for her moral conduct but not a certificate of sanctification. For large and small responsibilities alike we are obliged to face Divine law to consolidate our titles of worthiness in eternal life."

And, in a significant tone of voice, Aulus added:

"Let us recall the words of the Master: 'Much will be asked of those who much have received.'"

The conversation during the service had offered me sufficient material for meditation. The Mentor's valuable observations regarding mediumship further caused me to maintain silence and reflect.

The same was not true of my companion. The fluidic mirror, which the spiritual benefactors used to get information to answer questions quickly, displayed scenes of ill and anguished people. The delicate instrument worked perfectly, yet Hilario asked our mentor to explain it.

"It is a television managed by resources from our sphere."

"Does the mirror display the physical body or the soul?" Hilario inquired.

"The very soul. By examining the perispirit, information is received and conclusions reached. Many times it is imperative to analyze certain cases that have been presented meticulously; moreover, we then get aid from distant helpers.

"Spiritual workers are distributed through diverse regions where they capture the images and synchronize them with the receptor apparatus. The television[11] that extends itself over the world offers a similar idea, although our transmissions are much simpler, exact and instantaneous."

My colleague thought hard and then asked:

"Let us imagine that someone formulates a question to the one in charge of the mediumistic mandate and that the response is delayed. Let us imagine that the interested party situated at a distance, discarnates and remains, in Spirit, as occurs on many occasions, in a home or hospital bed, although already free of the physical body. In a case like this, does the reply from the spiritual benefactors refer to an incarnate?"

"This could occur in various circumstances," added the mentor, "since the service is not automatic or miraculous. We participate in a spirit of cooperation and goodwill, but success depends on mutual assistance, since fixing one piece does not fix the entire machine.

"The officials that receive this information demand efficiency on the part of those who transmit it. Many times, although being at a great distance, the suffering one is shown to those who propose to do the rescue. Due to the large number of requests, the Samaritans cannot judge if they are receiving

---

[11]**N.T.**: As a reminder to the reader, this book was written in 1955, which explains the above reference to the television.

information regarding an incarnate or discarnate. This occurs, in particular when they have not had vast experience. In certain situations, the needy require intensive assistance in a fraction of a minute. Therefore, any error of this kind is perfectly admissible."

"But would this not perturb the service of faith?" asked Hilario. "If we were the incarnates, would we not judge this as a useless response sent to a dead person?"

"No, Hilario, we cannot situate this question in these terms. The individual who seriously seeks faith, finds clear and quiet comprehension a gift without concerning himself or herself with superficial contradictions."

The mentor meditated an instant and observed:

"Moreover, if the consultants are frivolous and of poor faith, approaching the mediumistic task with incredibility and spiritual indifference, the results serve as a just harvest of the thorns they planted. They abuse the generosity and patience of friendly Spirits and attract denial and mental torture. The individual who throws mud in a clean fountain cannot expect to draw pure water from it."

Hilario, satisfied, became silent.

Two pass-givers were assisting patients in a room close by. While Ambrosina and the orators fulfilled their edifying duties, we turned toward the service of the magnetic passes, seeking additional knowledge.

17

The Service of Passes

We entered and found ourselves in a balmy and luminous ambient. An elderly gentleman and a respectable lady took notes in a small notebook. Spirits involved in healing services surrounded them. Pointing to the two mediums, our mentor informed us:

"These are Clara and Henrique, who are dedicated to the task of rendering assistance under the guidance of the spiritual friends who direct them."

"Why is this place so radiant?" – ventured Hilario with curiosity.

"In this room," explained Aulus affectionately, "we perceive sublime mental energies from the majority of the persons who, in love and confidence, use magnetic assistance. Here we possess a kind of inner altar created by the thoughts, prayers and aspirations of those who look for us to bring out the best they have to offer."

We did not have time for a long conversation. Clara and Henrique were now in prayer, surrounded by a halo of light. They were almost separated from their body and they appeared to be in direct contact with the benefactors present. Naturally, they themselves were not aware of this.

Serene and self-assured, they absorbed the invigorating forces into the depth of their souls. They knew that prayer kept them in communication with invisible and profound fountain of luminous energy.

Standing shoulder to shoulder, afflicted people stood murmuring in front of the closed door waiting for the preparations to finish. The two mediums, however, appeared to be spiritually distant, absorbed in the company of brotherly Spirits, registering their instructions by intuition.

From the radiations of Henrique's magnetism one could immediately perceive his superiority over his companion. Of the two, he was the central point. Because of this, positioned at his side was the spiritual mentor responsible for the task ahead.

Aulus embraced him affectionately and introduced him to us. Brother Conrado, our new friend, embraced us warmly. He informed us that the service would be open to us so that we could learn what we might from it. Our mentor invited us to be comfortable and authorized us to direct to Conrado whatever questions we had in mind. Hilario, who at no time repressed his spontaneity, respectfully began his questioning:

"Brother Conrado, do you come here frequently?"

"Yes, the Institution services the sick two nights a week."

"Only to the incarnates that are ill?"

"No, not exactly. We take care of the needy of whatever nature."

"Can you rely on many to cooperate?"

"We integrate a team of auxiliary workers, according to the organization established by the mentors from the Superior Spheres."

"Do you mean that in a Spiritist center, such as this one, there are spiritual collaborators enrolled as doctors and nurses in an ordinary hospital on Earth?"

"Exactly. We are all far from spiritual perfection and our success depends upon experience, time, accuracy and responsibility from the faithful worker

189

toward the obligations assumed. The Law cannot underestimate the rules of logic."

"What about the mediums: are they always the same ones?"

"Yes! In justifiable situations they can have substitutes, though there may be problems that result from adjusting to the new influences." My colleague directed a questioning glance toward the incarnate companions that remained in prayers and continued:

"Do our friends prepare themselves for the task through prayers?"

"Without a doubt. Prayer produces prodigious forces from the vigorous mental energy that it attracts. Through prayer, Clara and Henrique expel from their own interior world the remaining somber impressions gathered during the common activity of their daily circle of struggle. They then absorb from our plane the renewing substances with which they replenish themselves in order to succeed in working, efficiently, in favor of our neighbor. In this way they can assist and end up being firmly assisted."

"Does this mean that they should not fear becoming exhausted?"

"Not at all. Just as we, they do not appear here under the pretense of being the recipients of the benefits, but rather, as beneficiaries who receive in order to give. Prayer, along with the recognition of our small merits, places us in a position as simple links in a rescue chain that originates in the Heavens. Here we are, in this room consecrated to an Evangelical mission and under the inspiration of Jesus, somewhat similar to an electric outlet that allows the force that is not its own to produce energy and light."

Hilario smiled, satisfied with the clear explanation. Conrado put his arms over Henrique's shoulders in order to remind him of the established work schedule. The medium, in spite of not registering the gesture consciously, immediately walked over to the door and opened it to the needy ones who were waiting behind it.

A large group of incarnates and discarnates congregated at the entrance, as the companions of the house guided their movements. When Conrado began his tasks, we rejoined our mentor.

Both mediums started work. Patients of all kinds entered the room with great hope and most of them left contented after being treated. Clara and Henrique's hands radiated luminous sparks that gave vigor and well-being to the patients. In the majority of cases, they did not have to touch the patient's body with their hands. Magnetic resources applied at close range penetrated the aura of the sick, provoking sudden changes.

The pass-givers were as two human batteries that, upon contact with Brother Conrado and his collaborators, were able to spread a variety of rays flowing from their hands after passing over their heads. The display of lights at the scene was truly fascinating. Hilario, upon noting this, asked our mentor:

"Why does the energy transmitted by our spiritual friends first pass through the heads of the mediums?"

"Here as well," answered Aulus, "we cannot underestimate the importance of the mind. Thought plays a decisive role in healing. If the medium does not have faith and good will, he or she will not succeed in receiving the friendly Spirits who work upon these areas."

"Meanwhile, there are many people who also are endowed with magnetic energy but unconcerned with morality!" I interjected.

"Yes," agreed the mentor, "you are referring to the common hypnotizers who are often conveyers of exceptional energy. Their demonstrations are beautiful, impressive and convincing, but mainly it is pure phenomena and does not achieve edifying accomplishments in the spiritual field. Remember, Andre, that everyone has magnetic potential but it expresses itself differently."

"Yet such professionals also cure!" said my companion furthering my observations.

"Yes, they can also cure; however their cure is accidental. When the patient is worthy of spiritual assistance, spiritual friends intervene to assist he or she.

However, those that take advantage of this fountain of energy and exploit it for their personal gain, generally lower themselves interfering with unknown forces. They violate these forces, guided solely by vanity or an inferior ambition. They frequently encounter entities with which they have affinity, submerging, thereby, in difficult situations that there is no need to mention. If their character is too weak to pose a barrier to vicious influences, they end up devoured by energies stronger than theirs. There are an immense number of powerful spiritual hypnotizers who, through their ignorance and cruelty, are the initiators of the most severe cases of obsession."

After a pause, he smiled and added:

"In nature, the serpent possesses the greatest hypnotic power."

"Then to cure, certain attitudes of the spirit are indispensable?" asked Hilario.

"Without a doubt we cannot succeed without a noble heart and a pure mind exercising love, humility, and a living faith, in order that the rays of the Divine Will can penetrate and flow from us for the benefit of others. To cure effectively, this is pivotal."

"Moreover, for a task of this nature, would we not require people who have made special studies?"

"It is important to clarify," said Aulus with conviction, "that regardless of the task, lack of study means stagnation. Every collaborator who resists learning, refusing to incorporate new knowledge, fatally condemns oneself to activities of a lower level. But regarding the magnetic assistance such as it that is administered here, the task is of pure solidarity, and requires an ardent desire to aid, via invocation of prayer. Every prayer born of sincerity and a well-fulfilled duty, with moral respectability and clean sentiments, bears an incommensurable power. Therefore, all dignified and devoted people can with the aid of a prayer attract the sympathy of the venerable magnetizers of the Spiritual Plane, who then will utilize them to promote goodness. We do not practice spectacular hypnotism, but rather offer a place for healing, in which the mediums transmit the benefits that they receive, without presuming themselves to be the originators of healing. Wherever humility and love surge, Divine assistance is absolute and immediate."

The healing task about to begin within the efficient and quiet environment required our attention. Clara and Henrique, who were under the providential assistance of Conrado and his collaborators, affectionately greeted the patients who entered two at a time. Cruel executioners accompanied the obsessed individuals; however, as the mediums applied their hands over the cortical region the perpetrators immediately moved away. Unfortunately the majority of them rapidly went back to their victims after the treatment.

Reviewing our observations, we agreed that some of the patients had not achieved even a minimum of improvement. Magnetic radiations were not penetrating their organic vehicles. Registering these observations, Hilario quickly asked how this could happen.

"They lack confidence," clarified the mentor.

"Is faith indispensable, then, for them to receive the assistance they require?"

"Oh yes! In photography we require a negative to hold the image, and in electricity a wire for the transmission of the electric current. In spiritual assistance, the one in need requires faith to present a "favorable tension." We are not referring to religious fanaticism or to the blind faith of ignorance, but rather to an attitude of intimate assurance, with reverence and submission to Divine Laws, under whose wisdom and love we seek support. Without devotion and respect, we cannot take advantage of the imponderable resources that are offered to us for our own good. A heart that jeers at faith creates an icy barrier around the soul."

Hilario became quiet, reflecting on the simple and beautiful lesson.

To help us towards the goal of our study, Aulus allowed us to observe the treatment directly. We agreed that it would be interesting to examine one of the cases before us. He approached an elderly lady who had just entered in search of assistance, and with Conrado's permission, he suggested that we examine her as attentively as possible. The lady, while awaiting her encounter with Clara, stood with great difficulty. Her stomach was distended and her face showed pain.

"Observe the liver," Aulus said.

The organ was dilated, characteristic of people who suffer from cardiac insufficiency. The hepatic cells appeared as a vast beehive working with enormous difficulty. The congested gall bladder brought my attention to the intestines. The compressed bile reached the spleen, infecting the blood, and the common bile duct was not functioning. A cursory examination of the ocular mucous membrane confirmed my impression: all evidence indicated the woman suffered from jaundice[12].

After listening to me, Conrado affirmed:

"Yes, it is complex jaundice. It has its origin in a terrible fit of anger, which affected our friend in her home. Allowing herself to be controlled by anger, she developed an obstinate hepatitis, which resulted in jaundice."

---

[12]N.T.: jaundice – a yellowing of the skin, usually showing up in the whites of the eyes, fingernails, and other lightly pigmented parts of the body surface. There are three main causes: 1) accumulation of a breakdown product (called bilirubin) of excessive destruction of red blood cells (bruises often have localized jaundice in the early stage of healing), 2) a failure of the liver to remove the normal amounts of bilirubin, or 3) failure of elimination of bilirubin via the bile that is normally made in the liver and dumped into the intestine as a waste product.

"And how can she be assisted?"

Conrado, placing his hand over the forehead of the medium, sent a radiant current of energy that inspired her to move her hands over the patient, from the top of her head to the infirmed liver. We noticed that the encephalic cortex was covered by a luminous substance, which descended as fine threads to reach the visceral area. The woman's countenance displayed an undeniable expression of relief. She left visibly satisfied, promising to return to continue the treatment.

Hilario fixed his inquiring eyes on the mentor, who was amicably accompanying us, and asked:

"Will our sister be cured?"

"It is impossible," said Aulus in a fatherly manner. "Many organs and vessels are affected. Her healing requires time."

"Then what will be the basis of her cure?"

"Pass is a transfusion of energies that alters the entire cellular field. Even Science teaches us that the atom is not the indivisible component of matter, but rather prior to it are sub-atomic principles, and prior to these principles, is thought. In Nature, everything originates in the Spirit. If we renew our thoughts, everything within us is modified. In magnetic healing, the sending and receiving of spiritual resources helps the patient, so that one can help oneself. The enlivened mind is able to renew the microscopic organisms in the body and healing begins. Pass has a decisive influence in healing when received with respect and confidence."

"And can it be given at a distance?"

"Yes, as long as there is harmony between the one who administers it and the recipient. In this case, several spiritual companions collaborate to promote its realization. Moreover, silent prayer is the best vehicle for healing energy."

Around us the service continued. Aulus thought our presence might overtax Conrado's concentration and that we should leave, since we had already grasped the teachings that we desired. We said our farewells to the supervisor, and returned to the main salon in order to continue our lessons.

18
Margin Notations

Ambrosina continued receiving psychograph messages directed to those present. One of the orators, under the influence of a spiritual benefactor, was emphasizing that to merit blessings, we need to renew our thoughts and adjust them to Divine Laws.

Some incarnates continued to remain sleepy and impermeable, hypnotized by the capricious obsessing Spirits nearby. Meanwhile, many discarnates with some understanding were listening attentively and sincerely to the consoling teaching.

Gabriel, with bright penetrating eyes, firmly presided. Nothing, no matter how small, escaped from his perception. A slight signal from him caused enraged entities to change their attitude; with a simple gesture patients were assisted. He commanded strongly and assuredly, performing tasks with harmony and order.

We looked at the enormous table from which the directions were given and followed with equilibrium. Observing the medium in constant activity with the work props at hand, Hilario asked our mentor:

"Why are there so many personal messages from the friendly Spirits?"

"They are responses to the companions' questions that elicited their assistance and sympathy."

"Are these responses definite solutions?" asked my colleague.

"No, not really," the mentor clarified with conviction. "Between help and solution there is always a range in which problems can arise. After all, each of us presents his or her own enigmas and abnormalities."

"If that is so, why are there so many communications? If the discarnates cannot offer a balm for the torments of their incarnate brothers, why leave the door open between them and us?"

"We need cooperation for each step we take in life" replied Aulus gravely. "No matter how many years we live, physical existence is a short learning period. In addition, Earth is where we realize our evolvement through daily struggles. Within the principle of cause and effect, we acquire experiences that enrich our individuality and prepare us for higher spheres.

"The mind, truly, is like a traveler seeking an angelic state. Yet, it cannot advance without help. No one lives alone. A great number of the so-called dead will undergo new corporeal experiences and, therefore, must aid their living companions.

"The Law commands that wisdom rescues ignorance, and the more evolved aid those less righteous. A person that cooperates with advanced and benevolent Spirits attracts a precious congeniality for the spiritual life. Similarly, the friendly entities that assist the reincarnates facilitate their tomorrow, when they will return to terrestrial struggle."

"Yes, I understand," exclaimed Hilario gratefully. "We are accustomed to receiving decisive and absolute solutions to our problems from Heaven."

"This attitude," emphasized the mentor, "is due to an old mental vice, which is prevalent on the planet. In contrast, Jesus, the spiritual Governor of the Earth, aided the sick and the afflicted without removing their fundamental problems.

"The wealthy Zaqueus, honored by Jesus' visit, felt obliged to modify his conduct. Mary of Magdalene, who received His kind attention, was not free from the arduous battle for inner renovation. Lazarus, resurging from the shadows of the sepulcher, was not exonerated from death.

"He distinguished Paul of Tarsus with a personal call at the gates of Damascus, yet, he still had to sacrifice in order to fulfill his mission. We cannot expect discarnates to be free of all human struggles. This would eliminate the tasks that sustain the server and impede the lessons of the student in need of light."

At this stage, not far from us, a woman was thinking:

"My son! My son! If you are not dead, visit me! Come! Come! I am dying of anguish. I miss you. Say a word so we can understand one another. If all is not over, come close to the medium and communicate. It is impossible that you could have no pity!" A cavernous voice spoke these bitter, inarticulate phrases.

A slight sound behind us attracted our attention. A young man discarnate presented himself in a pathetic condition and, dominated by a great attraction, approached the sad woman. From his mouth came moving words:

"Mother! Mother!" – he shouted and knelt at her lap as if he were a tormented child. "Do not abandon me. Here I am. Listen to me: I did not die! Forgive me! Forgive me! I am a renegade, a failure! I sought death when I should have lived for your affection! Now I clearly see what the suffering is. I wish I could annihilate myself forever, so great is the shame in my heart."

The woman could not perceive the perturbed image; however, she felt his presence through an indescribable anxiety that compressed her chest. Two collaborators approached and took the young man from his mother's lap. We stood near the mentor who had hurried to rescue the lady, who was drenched in tears. She clamored mentally:

"Would it not be better to follow him? To die and rest! My dear son! I want my dear son!"

Aulus applied magnetic passes, after which the unfortunate lady felt a great relief. Soon after he informed us:

"Let us review this poor battered mother's case. Her son committed suicide a few months ago and she is still in pain. In her affectionate devotion, she seeks his manifestation without realizing what she is asking for, as her son's desperate situation constitutes a horrible martyrdom for her. For this reason she cannot receive his words directly. By undergoing this spiritual work, however, she will acquire energy that will gradually renew her."

"Of course," added Hilario intelligently, "this will not resolve her anguish, but it will tone her strength to recover."

"Yes, indeed." – agreed Aulus.

I considered: "Mediumship today is similar to the prophecies of the past."

"Yes," agreed Aulus quickly, "with the difference being that mediumship today is a concession of God to humanity that reflects the maturity of human understanding. Mediumistic phenomenon is not new, only the form in which it is disseminated. Different creeds existing for centuries were paralyzed with the spectacle of exterior demonstrations, making celestial revelations incomprehensible.

"Christianity in particular, which should be the simplest and most amplified school of faith, has long subscribed to temple rituals. It is imperative to liberate its principles from these to be of value to the world. These principles benefit from today's scientific findings. For this reason, the unseen government of this planet brought out in the open the notion of eternity, via the survival of the soul, to awaken the anesthetized minds of the public.

"This is how we see Jesus now: not as a founder of rituals and dogma, but as the true redeemer of human souls. Being an instrument of God in excellence, He utilizes mediumship to enhance His doctrine of love.

"On many occasions, He restored the sick and pacified the afflicted. He was in contact with the so-called dead. Some of these were nothing but suffering souls who vampirized the obsessed Besides talking with Moses, who was materialized on Mount Tabor, He himself appeared as the great resurrected one, bequeathing a vacant sepulcher to mankind. He accompanied His disciples with unblemished love, so that they would continue their apostleship."

Hilario displayed the smile of a student quite satisfied with the lesson and exclaimed:

"Oh yes, now I am beginning to understand."

The reunion was coming to a close. Our mentor perceived that Gabriel was about to write a closing message and respectfully asked him to explain a few concepts regarding mediumship. Gabriel graciously consented. Ambrosina paused briefly for her own recuperation.

The director of the reunion called for silence. He had barely reached a reverent tranquility when the conductor of the Center took control of the medium and, holding her arm, wrote rapidly. In minutes, Gabriel's message was finished. The medium arose and read it aloud:

"Dear friends," said the mentor, "do not seek in mediumship the false key to certain inadequate arrangements of the Earth, but rather the correct path that adjusts us for a superior life.

"It is necessary to renew our concepts regarding mediums to avoid turning them into oracles and fortunetellers, thus forgetting the duties that lead us toward purification.

"With Spiritism, Jesus returns to the world and invites us to achieve our improvement through constructive and incessant work. According to the law of cooperation, let us accept the affectionate hand of a friend to overcome anguishing trials. Let us not forget, however, that each of us brings unique problems and needs that are not transferable.

"As incarnates or discarnates we all traverse the extensive field of experiences and trials that harmonize with the imperatives of our spiritual growth. For this reason, one cannot attribute to mediums obligations that we must address ourselves, nor should we expect mediumship to function miraculously. We alone must make the arduous effort for our own ascension, with regard to the responsibilities that our higher conscience imposes on us.

"You may fall into laziness and ask: If Spiritism and mediumship cannot resolve our problems definitively, what are they doing in humanity's religious sanctuaries?

"Spiritism and mediumship contain the pure thought of Christ and assists us in understanding the truth with greater discernment. Through them we receive exact information regarding the law of compensations, the afflictive problems of the soul, of destiny and of pain. They allow us to perceive in a small way the infinite dimensions toward which we are evolving. From them we receive, above all, the light with which to overcome the dark gloomy labyrinths of death, so that we can finally associate with the cosmic conscience.

"Once we have reached similar formulas of reasoning, we will ask you: Do you believe that it would be of little importance to reveal the greatness of Justice? Do you admit that it is worthless to discover life with its limitless facets of evolution and eternity?

"Let us then revere Spiritism and mediumship as two living altars in the temple of faith. Through these, we can contemplate the sphere of meditations that pertains to Earth and finally understand that the glory reserved for the human spirit is sublime and infinite in the divine kingdom of the universe."

The psychograph communication included other matters, and after the reading was over, a brief prayer was offered in appreciation. While the assistant freely renewed the conversation, Hilario and I drew our thoughts inward to better learn the lesson.

19

Telepathic Control

We were preparing to bid farewell when a pleasant discarnate lady approached us complimenting the mentor with respectful affection. Aulus took charge of the introduction.

"This is our sister Teonilia, one of our diligent companions in the task of assistance."

The new friend gently returned our salutations and explained to the mentor what brought her here. She told us that Anesia, a devoted companion of this institution, was going through a difficult trial.

In addition to the usual preoccupations with her three daughters, and her essential assistance to her sick mother who was on the verge of discarnating, Anesia was going through a tremendous personal battle. Her husband Jovino was infatuated with another woman. He was negligent in his household obligations and appeared completely disinterested in her and their daughters. He had returned to the wild extravagances of his youth as if he had never assumed the role of a father.

Day and night he was controlled by the thoughts of this new woman, who was trapping him with her enticing lies. At home, during his professional activities and in his public life, this woman prevailed, controlling his unwary mind. The unfortunate man was transformed into an authentic obsessed individual, under the constant effects of someone senseless of his responsibility.

Could Aulus intercede? Wouldn't it be justified to remove her influence, as one would operate to excise a cancer? The mentor listened calmly and speak precisely:

"I know Anesia and I hold her in high esteem. For months I wanted to visit her but I have not had the opportunity. Of course I will not refuse to extend to her fraternal assistance, yet, it is not proper to take drastic measures without a clear observation of the case.

"We all know that obsession between discarnates and incarnates is a mental illness which may call for lengthy treatment. Although he appears robust, who knows if poor Jovino is not in the position of a hypnotized bird?"

"From what I can perceive," added the speaker, "I see only a dedicated man compromised and menaced by a perverse woman."

"Oh no!" interrupted the mentor. "Do not qualify her in such a manner. Above all, it is imperative to consider her an unfortunate sister."

"Yes, yes, I agree," exclaimed Teonilia. "In any case, I beg for your charitable intercession. Anesia has been a providential collaborator in our work and I could not be satisfied doing nothing.

"We shall do what is feasible, but it is vital that we analyze the past in order to reach the correct conclusions regarding the roots of this association," said Aulus.

Assuming a grave tone of voice, the mentor announced:

"Could Jovino be returning to his past inclinations? Could this be a redeeming trial but one he now cannot resist?"

Teonilia, silently, made a humble gesture while Aulus caressed her shoulders:

"Let us be optimistic and confident. Tomorrow, at nightfall, count on my being at Anesia's home. We shall observe and study closely what we must do."

Our friend expressed her gratitude with a smile and bid us farewell.

When we were alone and returning to our temple of work and study, Aulus invited us to continue our observations. The matter revolved around the reciprocal problem between two Spirits. We would have the opportunity of examining important yet common mediumship phenomena.

The next day, we traveled together and arrived at our destination by nightfall. Teonilia waited for us at the porch that, although not luxurious, was very comfortable. A small rose garden at the entrance demonstrated the beautiful sentiments of its residents.

Guided by our friend, we entered the house. The family was having dinner. A young lady was attentively serving a good-looking older gentleman. At his side were three girls, the youngest of whom was fourteen or fifteen years old and full of spring's grace.

The explanation of the previous night voided our need of new information; however, Aulus clarified:

"Here are Anesia and Jovino, and their three daughters, Marcina, Marta and Marcia."

The family's conversation was pleasant but Jovino appeared unnatural. The children's sweet observations did not bring even a weak smile to him. In spite of everything, the more the father expressed his discontent, the happier and more tender the mother became, encouraging the conversation of the two older daughters regarding humorous incidents at the store in which they worked.

After dinner, the wife spoke to the youngest and affectionately recommended:

"Marcia, dear daughter, return to grandmother's bedroom and wait for me. She should not be left alone."

The young girl gladly obeyed and later Marcina and Marta retired to an adjoining room where they continued their intimate conversation.

Anesia worked silently as she put things away in the kitchen cabinets while her husband sat on the sofa and read the evening newspapers. Upon noticing that the husband was getting up again as if to depart, she looked at him inquiringly, and delicately asked:

"Should we wait for you today?"

"Today, today…" repeated the husband without looking at her.

"Yes, and perhaps a little later we could all say our prayers together," said Anne.

"Prayers? What for?"

"Jovino, I truly believe in the power of prayer and I am sure that we have never needed them as much as we do now."

"I do not agree with you," and smiling, but with sarcasm, he continued, "and I don't have time to adjust to your beliefs. I have important issues to deal with. I plan to review an excellent business proposition with some friends."

At that moment, however, an image of the other woman arose unexpectedly before his eyes projected from a distance, appearing and disappearing intermittently. Jovino immediately became more distracted and annoyed. He now viewed at his wife with an ironic indifference, demonstrating a profound spiritual harshness.

Intrigued by this scene, we heard Anesia, inspired by Teonilia, say:

"Jovino, don't you agree that we are distant from one another when it is so important for us to be united?"

"Come on! Your notions are sentimental and ridiculous. They might have been justified twenty years ago when we were silly students!"

"No, you do not understand. Our home and our daughters concern me."

"As for me, I don't see any reason to torture myself. I believe my home is well provided for and I am not indifferent to the interests of the family. My business is doing well but we require funds. For that reason, I cannot waste time in religious matters, where petitions are directed to God, who, undoubtedly, should be very satisfied to live in Heaven and not have to remember the Earth at all."

Anesia was going to answer but her husband's attitude was so fragrantly mocking that she did not reply. The head of the family straightened his lively colored tie and slammed the door as he left. His embarrassed companion dropped onto an old sofa silently crying and started to think.

"Business! Business! What lies upon lies! Another woman, yes! A heartless woman who does not see our problems! Debts, work, exhausting efforts! Our home mortgaged, my elderly mother at the point of death! Our little daughters fighting for their own existence!"

Meanwhile, her reflections radiated through the narrow living room and reached us. We saw once again the image of the woman that rose in front of Jovino also appear close to the sad wife, as if desiring to pierce her heart with invisible darts of anguish. In fact, Anesia felt an indefinable discomfort.

She did not see the strange and undesirable visitor, but she sensed her presence as an uncontrollable mental tribulation. Suddenly, her calm meditative state turned into tormenting thoughts.

"I remember her now," she reflected in desperation. "I know her. She is a perverse woman, the cause of disturbance in our home. Jovino has changed. He is abandoning us little by little. He even appears to detest prayer. Ah! What a horrible being. She is an adversary that works herself into our existence like a reptile. If I could, I would crush her under my feet, but today my religious faith protects my heart from violence."

While Anesia's thoughts were filled with animosity, the image projected at a distance started coming closer and intensifying, as if she were materialized in the atmosphere, causing the distraught wife greater discomfort. The woman that dominated Jovino was embodied before our eyes. And both women, now declared enemies, commenced a mental battle of sad thoughts, harsh words and reciprocal accusations.

The tormented wife started to feel uncomfortable physical sensations. Blood rushed to her head causing a strange pain. The more the rebellious and bitter her thoughts, the greater her physical imbalance. Teonilia caressed her with great affection and informed the mentor:

"For many weeks this encounter has repeated itself daily. I fear for our companion's health."

Aulus commenced to apply magnetic passes and the strange manifestations began to diminish until they disappeared completely. After completing Anesia's treatment, the mentor satisfied our curiosity:

"Jovino's yields easily to her strong telepathic control. When you consider that husband and wife live under the reciprocal influence, it is no wonder that Anesia suffers along with her husband the same control.

The poor child does not know how to protect herself by practicing unconditional forgiveness."

Intrigued, Hilario asked:

"Is this a common phenomenon?"

"Very common. It is the influence that incarnate souls exercise over each other that sometimes reaches a dangerous obsession. Millions of homes can be compared to a battlefield, where thoughts fight with thoughts, causing the most varied forms of anguish and repulsion."

"Is this within the domain of mediumship?"

'Yes, and I must add that because it operates synchronously, it is responsible for many types of mental alienation. Many times, the superior sphere place implacable adversaries of the past in the same home, family or institution in order to reconcile.

"But rarely do they succeed in overcoming the aversion that they feel for one another. Concentrated rays of antipathy are toxic and transform into magnetic venom capable of producing illnesses and even death. For this, it is not necessary that the persecution manifests itself visibly. When both sides feed on silent vibrations of cruelty, defiance, hatred, jealousy, violence and despair, they constitute destructive corrosives."

After a brief pause, the mentor continued:

"Thought exteriorizes itself and is projected to its target in the form of images and suggestions. When they are benign and edifying, and conform to the laws that guide us, they create harmony and happiness. When they are evil and demoralizing, however, they produce pain and ruin. Mental chemistry acts in the same way, being the base of all transformations, because we evolve in profound telepathic communion with all incarnates or discarnates that have affinity with us."

"And how can we resolve the problem of antipathy that someone has against us?" inquired my companion with great interest.

Aulus smiled and responded:

"The best way to eradicate the fire is to reduce its energy. Living fraternally shall always be the edifying remedy for these interferences. It is for this reason that Jesus Christ recommended that we love our enemies, help those who persecute us and pray for those that slander us. These are essential attitudes that guarantee peace and victory."

At that very moment Anesia checked her watch and stood up. It was 8:00pm, her usual time to pray with her ill mother. We accompanied her with a desire to join in her prayers.

20

Mediumship and Prayer

In a small room, a lady about 70 years old was having difficult breathing. The small Marcia, waving an improvised fan, was trying to keep cool. Next to the ill woman a Spirit with a disagreeable appearance wore a look of confusion and suffering. Because of his proximity and association with her, he aggravated her physical discomfort. The discarnate individual displayed evidence of mental alienation.

Anesia sat close to her mother, exhibiting an affectionate tenderness and trying to forget her personal problems. Aulus informed us fondly:

"Here we see our sister Elisa undergoing an advanced liberating process. She is living her last hours in her physical body."

"And who is the sad man at her bedside?" asked Hilario, pointing to the Spirit that was unaware of our presence.

"He is an unfortunate son of our dear friend, who departed from physical life many years ago. He was assassinated one night after an excessive use of alcohol. The mother, however, remembers him as a hero and invokes him incessantly, thereby attracting the poor man to her bed."

"Oh! But why?"

The mentor modified the tone of his voice and recommended serenity. "We shall analyze the case at the appropriate moment. It is Anesia's problem that requires our immediate attention."

Truly, the poor woman with a fatigued face caressed the patient affectionately, but Elisa appeared indifferent. Anesia started to cry.

"But why cry, mother? Grandmother is not worse." Hearing Marcia's soft voice impressed on us an indescribable tone of love. The young girl, who could not even remotely perceive the torture her mother felt, embraced Anesia lovingly and invited her to join in a prayer.

Anesia desired the presence of her older daughters, but Marcina and Marta said that they had to leave in a few minutes to go to a colleague's birthday. The housewife sat with the patient and, with her daughter's full attention, said a sentimental prayer.

As she prayed, a profound change took place inside her. The darts of sadness that lacerated her soul disappeared due to the soft rays of light vibrating outwardly from her heart. From that moment on, as if a light had been lit in absolute darkness, a few discarnate sufferers entered the room. They approached Anesia, as would patients awaiting their medication.

No one noticed our presence. Because of our curiosity, Aulus explained:

"They are companions who sense vibratory sensations identical to those of corporeal existence. In their present state they improve more rapidly with the assitance from incarnate companions, as their impressions are the same.

"Those who find themselves in a similar state within the radius of the action from our friend's prayers, receive the spiritual effluvia that emanates from them. Many are sensitive to goodness and, thirsting for inner evolvement, respond readily to the elevated appeal that reaches them Through the sublime power of prayer they receive enlightenment, consolation, aid and benefits."

"What great value is found in a seemingly insignificant act of faith."

The mentor caressed Hilario's forehead and continued:

"On Earth, human beings create enormous difficulties for themselves; however, death obliges them to return to simplicity and regenerate their own life."

Anesia opened her priceless book of Evangelical meditations, expecting her choice to be random. It was actually Teonilia, kindly watching all Anesia's movements, who chose the theme.

Anesia was surprised that the text concerned work and forgiveness. Being influenced by the spiritual mentor, Jovino's wife spoke humbly but with wisdom, regarding the necessity of service and constructive tolerance.

Unknowingly, she transmitted in a soft fluid voice the thoughts of Teonilia, who meanwhile tried to rescue Anesia's tormented heart. In an extended pause, Marcia intelligently said:

"Continue mother, continue. I have the impression that we are standing in front of a great multitude."

And, without realizing that she was preaching more for herself than the others, Anesia added:

"Yes, dear daughter, we are alone because grandmother is fatigued and does not hear us. This, however, is in appearance only, as many discarnate brothers are surely here close to us, accompanying us in our prayer."

Her comments renewed the enthusiasm of those present that desired light and thirsted for peace and moral reform. After the prayer ended, Marcia kissed her mother goodbye. She needed to rest for school the next day.

After making affectionate recommendations to the young girl, Anesia was left alone with her mother. She caressed her pale wrinkled face. She cuddled her moist head on the pillows and lay pensively at her side. Aulus gestured to Teonilia and exclaimed:

"Our time has come."

Cautiously, they applied passes to her head, concentrating magnetic energy lengthwise along the cortical cells. She did not reject the slight hypnosis that compressed her body and made her feel sleepy. After a few moments, her body controlled by sleepiness, she approached us out-of-body. However, she did not manifest sufficient consciousness in our plane, as we would have desired.

The affection for her husband, Jovino, constituted an obstinate preoccupation. She recognized Teonilia and Aulus as benefactors and, even though she appeared confused and preoccupied, directed a particularly affectionate glance at us. She wanted to see and hear her husband. Aulus decided to grant her wish.

Being held by the arms of the admirable friend, she walked as if she knew exactly how to find her husband. Aulus explained to us that souls who are linked together live united through magnetic ties that allow them overcome obstacles and distances.

In the large room of a nightclub, we surprised Jovino and the woman that we had known telepathically. They were part of a happy group and displayed an attitude of profound and intimate affection. Diverse Spirits unknown to us surrounded the group, forming a circle of vicious vampires. These Spirits could not perceive us. The group was animatedly making small talk.

Encountering her husband in this situation, Anesia shouted painfully and began to cry. We followed her as she retreated in pain and shock into the cool night air. The mentor embraced her as a loving father would.

She gradually became more composed, although suffering transformed her face. Aulus spoke affectionately:

"Dear sister, please take hold of yourself. You prayed so that you could receive spiritual assistance and we have answered your call. Cheer up! Don't lose hope."

"Hope?" replied the poor woman, whose face was bathed in tears. "I am the object of betrayal."

The conversation between them continued in a moving expressive tone.

"Betrayal by whom?"

"By my husband, who failed in his marriage promises."

"Do you believe that marriage is a simple excursion on Earth? Dear friend, the home is a school where souls reunite to achieve individual regeneration knowing that perfection is ours in the future. In educational establishments there are professors and students. Don't you know that the best ones should help those marching behind?"

Upon hearing Aulus' words, Anesia interrupted her laments. Yet, after looking at our mentor with intense confidence, she began sadly:

"But Jovino..."

Aulus interrupted her, adding:

"Are you forgetting that now is when your husband requires your understanding and affection? A woman should not always view her companion as the man she loves tenderly, but as a spiritual son, who needs to be guided with understanding and sacrifice. Equally, a husband should not always contemplate his wife as the flower of his dreams, but rather as a daughter of his heart, who ask for tolerance and kindness, so that she can be taken from darkness to light.

"Anesia, love is not just rosy happiness and the sweet response to sex. It is a light that shines in the heights, inspiring the renunciation and unconditional pardon of those we love. Jovino is like a plant that God conveyed into your hands, and you must be a gardener. The plant will be attacked by parasites or deadly worms; however, there is no reason to fear if the gardener is attentive and vigilant."

With the mentor's beautiful words, Anesia turned to him, as would a patient holding on to one's doctor, telling him in a supplicant tone:

"Yes, yes, I realize but, in the meantime, please don't leave me alone. I feel afflicted. What can I do about the woman that dominates him? In her I see the cause of the confusion and the bitterness of our home. She resembles a diabolic Spirit, fascinating and destroying him."

"Do not refer to her with such harsh words. She is also our sister, a victim of painful errors!"

"But how can I accept her? I can perceive her malignant influence. She seems to be an invisible serpent that brings terrible monsters to us. She has transformed our home and temple into a hell in which we can no longer understand one another. Now, everything is failure, disharmony and insecurity. What can I do about such a person?"

"We must feel compassion for her. Her awakening shall be a painful one"

"Compassion?"

"What reprisal could be better than that?"

"Wouldn't it be more justified to begin correcting her own errors? Wouldn't it be better to relegate her to the dark place that she deserves?"

Aulus held Anesia's wavering hand and continued.

"Let us abstain from judging. According to the lesson from our Master, love should be the only attitude to have toward our adversaries. Revenge, Anesia, is the soul of black magic. Evil over evil signifies the absolute eclipse of reason. And in the empire of the shadows, what can we expect but blindness and death?

"No matter how painful it is to think of this woman, consider her in your prayers and meditations as a sister requiring our fraternal help. As of yet, we have not achieved the integral memory of our past and we do not know what will occur to us in the future. Who could she have been in the past? Could she be someone that we have aided or hurt? Who will she be in the future? Our mother or our daughter?

"Do not condemn! Hatred is like a fire that consumes everything, but love knows how to put out the fire and reconstruct. According to the Law, righteousness neutralizes evil, which is ultimately transformed into the service of goodness. Although everything appears to conspire against your personal happiness, love and always help. Time will take care of dissipating the shadows that surround us, in accordance with the augmentation of our moral merit."

Anesia, resembling a resigned child, looked at the benefactor with limpid eyes that promised obedience. Aulus, caressing her, recommended:

"Return to your home and defend yourself with humility and forgiveness, work and prayer, kindness and silence. Your dear sick mother and your little girls claim your pure love, as well as our Jovino. He will return with more experience to the refuge of your heart."

Anesia raised her head, looked at the sky inundated with light, said a prayer of praise and immediately returned home. We witnessed her awakening again in her physical body with her soul renewed, almost happy. She dried her tears and anxiously tried to recall every point of the conversation she had with us. Although she only recalled fragments, she did feel comforted, without rebellion or bitterness. It was as if intangible hands had cleaned her mind, conferring a better comprehension of life.

She recalled with compassion Jovino and the woman that fascinated him, recognizing them as people needing tolerance and pity. A profound understanding now arose from her spirit The comprehension of the sister overcame the unbalance of the woman.

Anesia realized that it would be no good for her to rebel or be discouraged, since she should defend her home. Wouldn't establishing justice with her own hands bias her towards those she treasured in her heart? Scandal is the ruination of all happiness. Shouldn't she be thanking God for acting as a dignified wife? Yes, of course self-responsibility and discernment are not awakened in the poor woman that disturbed her husband. She requires, therefore, compassion and assistance, instead of criticism and harshness."

Consoled and satisfied, she prepared her mother's medication. Hilario, quite surprised, exalted the merits of prayer and then Aulus said:

"In all of our exchange with incarnates, from a tortured mediumship to an all glorious one, prayer is like a blessed light that assimilates superior mental forces, which aid us in redemption and ascension."

Signaling to the housewife now working in the room my colleague observed:

"We see, then, in our friend a beautifully developing mediumship."

"Just as occurs to millions of people," said the mentor, "she possesses appreciable mediumistic resources that can be used for good as well as evil. She now has the obligation of constructing within herself the same strength of knowledge and vigilance to be able to enjoy, in thought, the company of enlightened Spirits who can lead her to happiness."

229

"And through prayer she seeks to resolve the enigmas that torture her existence..."

Aulus smiling, added:

"We find here a precious teaching regarding prayer. Using prayer, Anesia could not modify the facts per se, but she did succeed in modifying herself. The actual difficulties were not altered. Jovino is still in danger, their home continues to be threatened in its fundamental morals, the elderly patient nears death;, and meanwhile, our sister received an expressive coefficient of energy that will allow her to accept the trials that she must endure, attempting to overcome them with patience and valor. A transformed Spirit, naturally transforms the circumstances."

The mentor, nevertheless, interrupted the explanations and reminded us that it was time to return. In response to a request from Teonilia, he examined Elisa and said that her death was imminent. I expressed my desire to examine Elisa's physical body, but the mentor reminded us of the late hour, promising to return with us on the following night to assist the elderly lady.

21

Mediumship on the Death Bed

The following night we returned to Anesia's home to help her sick mother. Elisa had taken a turn for the worse. We found her agitated, as if she would soon separate herself from the physical body.

The family doctor examined her body and his findings caused him to be preoccupied and disconsolate. He analyzed her exhausted heart with a stethoscope. The rise of the amount of urea indicated an alarming toxicity. He perceived that her physical resistance was near its end. Her delirium, however, puzzled him.

Elisa found herself a prisoner of a strange mental confusion. Overexcited and in anguish, she imagined that she was being followed by a man who intended to shoot her. She called for her long-dead son. She claimed to see serpents and spiders at the foot of her bed. Although she was sweating and pale, she made an effort to speak.

The doctor called Anésia to the side and discussed his evaluation. To meet this crisis, the patient should proceed with emergency measures and take medication; she would spend the night in pain. The uremia was advancing rapidly and her heart was like a ship without a helm; she could collapse at any moment.

Anesia listened to the doctor, wiping the tears that flowed from her eyes. She bid him farewell and began to pray, still dependent on Teonilia's influence, who was watching over her as if she were Anesia's Divine protector.

Without being able to explain it even to herself, serenity slowly took over her soul. She became calm, believing with faith, patience and certainty that the assitance from the superior plane would not fail her. Although not able to perceive the tenderness coming from her devoted friend, Anesia received comforting expressions in the form of sublime thoughts of hope and peace.

She paused, as she contemplated the elderly lady who asked in a pained voice for help, and noticed how slightly open the expressionless eyes were. A profound pity swept over her because of her great filial affection.

"Dear mother," she said affectionately, "do you feel better now?"

The mother took her by the hands as if she were a frightened child, and murmured:

"Dear daughter, I am not better because an assassin is after me. I don't know how to escape from him. Big spiders surrounded me. How can I escape?"

Then, immediately raising the tone of her voice, she screamed with painful inflexion, "Oh the serpents! They threaten me from the door! What is to become of me?" She tried to hide her face in her thin hands and made a vain attempted to raise her quivering head.

"Dear mother, please calm yourself!" begged her daughter, quite moved. "Let us confide in providence. Jesus is our vigilant Friend. Why not rely on His protection? You will recover. Observe attentively. Our room is peaceful."

The patient became somewhat calmer but her eyes reflected fear and lack of confidence. Asking Anesia to bend down, she whispered in her ear.

"I feel that Olimpio is with us. My son came down from Heaven to receive me. I do not doubt it. He is my son, yes ... my son."

The affectionate daughter believed her; however, she knew that her brother's presence would not be desirable, and said: "Why don't we join in prayer and plead for celestial assistance?"

Anesia assumed the role of interpreter for Teonilia, forcing herself to enfold the elderly lady with calming fluids. Aulus then invited us to observe the communion between the discarnate son and the poor mother. Olimpio, the young man who had been assassinated, was holding her, as a parasitic plant would asphyxiate a frail tree.

"Our friend," explained Aulus with affection, "supposes that her son is a guardian angel, when actually he is an unfortunate who allowed himself to be controlled by alcoholism even in death. An impenitent alcoholic, he died of a gunshot from an equally disoriented companion.

"Separated from his physical body and intensely involved in "delirium tremens," he did not have the strength necessary to recuperate. He continued in the company of those that prolonged the excesses he enjoyed. Invoked by his mother's memory, however, he approached this room in and is confused by her request.

"As she gradually separates from her physical body, our sister transfers her emotional field from the sphere of the flesh to this of the Spirit, compulsively suffering the pernicious influence from the entity whom she called to her side through her will and thoughts. They are two minds synchronized by the impressions. As weak as she is, she easily succumbs to the control of the young man, whose fear and disequilibrium are transmitted to her submissive and affectionate soul.

Analyzing the phenomenon, I asked if this could be compared to the mediumistic faculty of trance communication.

"Without a doubt," confirmed the mentor, "Elisa is attracting her son to her side during a profound passive state caused by her weak nervous condition. Lacking experience that could give her discernment and defense, she assimilates his mental energies and inner disharmony. While going through the slow process of death, she reflects his past memories and the terrible hallucinations that invade him now, since, his unfortunate son, as all victims of chronic alcoholism, experiences the consequences of uncontrolled libations."

"Heavens!" – exclaimed Hilario, compassionately. "How can we abandon the elderly patient experiencing a trial of this nature? Would this not be a tremendous injustice?"

"I agree with you that it is a lamentable scene," added Aulus. "No one, however, eludes the laws that direct our life. With the presence of her son, Elisa received what she was ardently seeking. It is true that she is an elderly lady nearing death, but she is also an imperishable and responsible Spirit managing mental values expressed and conjugated according to clear and definable principles."

And after a brief pause, the mentor continued:

"Many times we don't realize what we ask for and receive what we do not desire. In the end, however, there is always a gain because the Father permits us to draw what is valuable from every problem."

Aulus did not waste time in digressions. He conversed privately with Teonilia concerning the patient's program and accepting our collaboration, separated the young man by employing magnetism.

As soon as the unfortunate Olimpio left Elisa, we perceived an interesting phenomenon: Elisa, who had been talking animatedly, went into an absolute prostration as if she had been restrained. Observing our curiosity, Aulus explained:

"The presence of her discarnate son fed her mental excitement, which affected her nervous field. Now she can rely only on her own energies."

The patient emitted some guttural sounds, then immediately became quiet. In vain, Anesia tried to draw a word out of her. Elisa was able to see and hear but could not articulate a single phrase! She tried in vain to move her arms, due to the strong pain in her chest, but did not have enough strength. Aulus hurriedly tried to administer calming passes, but without result.

"It is the final constriction of the coronaries" he exclaimed, quite moved. "Elisa will not be able to resist. The myocardium no longer reacts to our magnetic energy. The angina process has reached its end."

I noticed that Elisa wanted to talk to her daughter, despite the uncontainable pain that she felt in the thorax, but her tongue would not obey.

She felt the time had come for her to take the journey to the tomb. As if a lightening had struck her mental trouble, in one of those moments that are worth centuries for the soul, she rapidly saw the past. Scenes from her childhood, youth and maturity appeared in her memory, as if she were being invited to a scrupulous examination of her conscience.

With her moments in the flesh numbered, she did not hesitate. Unable to communicate with her daughter, she wanted to say farewell to her elderly sister that lived far away. We could see her concentrating her thoughts in a supreme effort to satisfy this last desire.

Anesia remained under Teonilia's influence and perceived that her mother was reaching the end of her terrestrial existence. She embraced her affectionately, crying silently, and prayed. Elisa understood her daughter but could only shed tears in reply.

Fixing a painful and anxious look at her daughter, Elisa projected herself to our side, but the silver cord still attached her to her physical body.

While her arms and legs became taut, only one thought controlled her spirit: to bid goodbye to the only sister she had on Earth. With a wave of strength born of her will, she departed hurriedly and headed for the city in which her sister lived.

At Aulus's request, we followed her closely. Dozens of miles were covered instantaneously. We accompanied her into a small and darkened room, in which we saw a venerable elderly lady quietly sleeping.

"Matilde! Matilde!"

Elisa tried to awaken her quickly, but in vain. Conscious of the fact that she only had moments left she knocked on her sister's bed. Matilde then awakened, immediately entering into her sister's sphere of influence.

Elisa, distraught, tried to talk to her. Matilde, however, did not hear the words with her ears but through the mental waves of her brain in the form of thoughts hovering in her head. Straightening up, she said to herself: "Elisa has died."

Pointing to the two sisters, the mentor explained: "Here we have a common type of communication in cases of death. Due to the repeated occurrences, the scientists of the world are obliged to examine them. Some attribute these actions as telepathic transmission, while others see this as phenomenon of premonition. The Spiritist doctrine shows us the pure and simple truth that this is the direct communion between immortal souls."

"Can all persons, provided they desire it, accomplish these farewells when leaving the Earth?" asked my colleague.

"Yes, Hilario, you are correct when you say 'as long as they desire it'. Such communications at the instant of death are only achieved by those who concentrate their mental power on a cause of this kind."

We did not have time to prolong this conversation. Once liberated from the desire that disturbed her inwardly, Elisa returned to her house as if her distant body were requesting her presence (similar to that which occurs in a common out-of-body experience). Following her closely we noticed she was less emotionally affected, although quite fatigued.

In the familiar room she tried to recuperate her physical body by resorting to her old habits, as if reality were merely a strange dream, but she oscillated over her bed extremely tired and tormented, attached to her remains only by the narrow silver thread.

The recent discarnate, with oppressed soul, resisted the desire to rest that invaded her thoughts. She was unable to determine if she were alive or not. Other spiritual friends entered her room.

Aulus checked the time and added: "Let us return. There is no more to do here."

Hilario observed the silver cord that linked the rigid body with our newly liberated friend and asked: "Can we cooperate in trying to separate her from that annoying cord?"

"No," explained the mentor, "this bond has a specific function in the re-equilibrium of the soul. Death and birth are functions of eternal life, which require work and patience. Furthermore, there are companions who are specialized in the service of final liberation. They are responsible for this task."

Then, accompanying the mentor, we left Anesia's home. We had received a priceless lesson.

22

Emerging From the Past

In the company of Aulus, we returned to the second weekly meeting of the group presided by Raul Silva. Our mentor did not hide his attraction and confidence towards that group, due to its organization. Although the group of workers was the same of the previous night, the small row of patients was different.

Two women, each followed by her respective husband, and a gentleman bearing a fatigued expression were part of the latter group. Along with Celina's efficient collaboration, the mediums of the Center lent their help for those suffering Spirits lost in darkness.

Once the diverse problems related to the evening's program were resolved, one of the ill ladies fell into a convulsive crying fit, exclaiming:

"Who will help me? Who will help me?"

And while she pressed her hands to her chest, she added, in a moving tone:

"Coward! Why stab a defenseless woman? Will I be totally at fault? My blood will condemn your wretched deed."

With his habitual serenity, Raul moved close to her and consoled her affectionately.

"Dear sister, forgiveness is the remedy that nourishes our sick soul. Do not permit your desperation to subjugate your energies. To recall offenses is to remain in darkness. Let us forget the evil and let the light of goodness facilitate our path."

"Forget? Never! Do you know what it is to have a blade cut into your flesh? Do you know about the calamity of having a man suck the life from our existence and throwing us into misery, then taking pleasure afterward in spilling our own blood?"

"No one denies your right to justice, but wouldn't it be more prudent to uphold the declaration of Divine kindness? Which of us is without sin?"

"Wait, wait! It has been such a long time that I have done nothing but wait. In vain I attempt to recapture happiness. No matter how I try to break with the past, I live under the shadow of remembrances, as someone who carries on his or her chest the tomb of dead dreams. All of this because of the wicked one who ruined my destiny."

The poor child broke into sobs, while a discarnate not too far away observed her with great discouragement. Bewildered, Hilario and I directed a questioning glance at the mentor, who perceived our perplexity. The patient suffered in pain, despite the fact that the invisible woman whom she appeared to personify was not present.

"I do not see the Spirit that our sister interprets," said Hilario with curiosity.

"Yes," I said. "I see a sad discarnate near us. However, if he were telepathically linked to our sister, surely the message would have masculine characteristics, and not feminine, as we see. In addition, we do not notice any magnetic ties that indicate teledynamic fluids controlling the mind of the medium."

Aulus caressed the patient's tear-covered face and, as if he were analyzing her thoughts, explained:

"We are facing our companion's past. The sorrow and harshness, as well as the supposedly exotic personality that she manifests, stems from her. Facing her old enemy from our plane who still pursues her, she revives the painful experiences that occurred to her in a

European city during the past century and resumes the emotion of indomitable melancholy."

"She felt new hope in the present reincarnation. However, her battle started again as soon as she sensed the spiritual visit of her former executioner to whom she held ties of love and hate. This disturbed her mental life because her education is incomplete. It is a case that offers valuable teachings."

"Then, this means that..."

The mentor completed Hilario's thought: "Our sister's response to her painful experience was so strong that even the biological shock of rebirth, did not make her forget. She fixes herself on the memory, when her executioner is near, and acts as if she still lives in the past. When this happens, she takes on a different personality."

Smiling in a fatherly manner, he pondered:

"She has returned from the past to communicate with the present, because as she receives painful memories she concentrates her remembrances to where her thoughts were. To the common psychiatrist, she is solely a candidate for insulin or electro-shock therapy. For us, she is a spiritually ill patient with a tortured conscience that requires moral and cultural assistance to her inner transformation. Only this will assure her well-being."

I analyzed her carefully and concluded:

"Mediumistically speaking, we have here an authentic case of animism.[13] Our friend supposes she is giving a communication from a different personality when in truth she expresses her personal inner world."

"Could we then classify this as a case of unconscious mystification?" asked Hilario.

Aulus meditated a minute and pondered: "Many companions working to establish a new era under Spiritism are converting the theory of animism into a trick that impedes their reaching the good they seek. Therefore, it is not acceptable to adopt the word *mystification*, 'unconscious or subconscious,' to explain this phenomenon.

"The manifestation derives from sentiments in her past. From these, she extracts depressing impressions and externalizes them. The poor woman realizes this while in a somnambulistic state in which she concentrates all her attention on the memories referred to, and transforms them into a unique wound. This causes her to lack concern for her present responsibilities. We face a mentally ill patient who requires our great affection for her recuperation. To cure her uneasiness, however, a technical diagnosis is

---

[13]**N.T.:** Animism: situation in which the medium's subconscious mind, rather than a spiritual individuality, is the source of a mediumistic message. The term is also used to identify religious practices based on the belief that all living things have a soul. However, only the former notion is recognized in the Spiritist literature. (Source: Glossary from Allan Kardec's *"The Spirits' Book"* by Allan Kardec Educational Society, 2002).

not enough. She needs, rather, to feel fraternal warmth and friendly assistence."

Aulus paused briefly, while he caressed the patient. As Raul Silva continued talking to her and consoled her, our mentor told us, kindly:

"She should be treated with the same attention that we give to the communicating Spirits that suffer. She is also an immortal Spirit that beseeches our attention and understanding to restore her equanimity. The idea of a mystification would give us a disrespectful attitude regarding her moral illness. For this reason, it is imperative to fill our hearts with love so that we may aid and comprehend her.

"A tactless counselor would only aggravate the problem. On the pretext of serving truth, he would impose an inopportune correction instead of providential assistance. First, it is necessary to remove the evil, and afterward fortify the victim so that she can learn how to defend herself. Fortunately, Raul assimilates the spiritual energy of goodness that reigns here, being an ideal attendant for situations of this nature."

Hilario, feeling as uplifted as I was with the teachings we heard, asked respectfully:

"And can we consider her a medium?"

"Why not? A defective instrument can be repaired and restored to service. Naturally, it is necessary to work patiently and charitably to save her.

Our sister should be heard as if she were that unfortunate woman of yesterday. As such, we should receive her so that she can use the moral remedy we offer. Only then, she will finally be disassociated from the past that haunts her. There is no contradiction here, since the former woman undoubtedly exists within her. This personality was not sufficiently eclipsed by a new reincarnation, as it should have. She was reborn in flesh without renovating herself in spirit."

The mentor submerged in his own reflections, and then spoke:

"She represents thousands of other souls. How many beggars on Earth pull off the torn mantle of the brief nobility that had covered them in the past? How many slaves of poverty and pain drag with them the vanity and pride of the powerful beings that they once were? How many souls travel from the cradle to the grave transporting invisible sores of aversion and hatred toward their own families, who were their rude adversaries in prior existences? We can all fall into similar states if we do not learn to forget evil and march incessantly with goodness."

At this point Raul Silva, in his role of capable psychologist, invited the patient to join in prayer. It was up to her to beg the Heavens for the opportunity to receive the blessings of forgetfulness. It was up to her to erase the past from her imagination to achieve calm and find peace. Raul, quite touched, invited her to repeat in his company the sublime words of the Lord's Prayer.

The poor woman prayed meekly with him. After the prayer she appeared more at ease. The good friend translating the mentor's collaboration begged the woman to consider that to regain peace it is important, above all, to forgive her enemies. Subsequently, the patient, whose face bathed in tears, disassociated from the impressions that tied her to the past and returned to her normal state.

While Raul applied passes to comfort her, the mentor commented:

"There can be no other assistance to offer her. With this type of spiritual therapy she will improve little by little, leading her self control to return, and making her capable of engaging in valuable mediumistic tasks later."

We wanted to continue the analysis of the case, but another patient unexpectedly fell into an agitated trance and it was necessary to continue to study productively.

23

Fascination[14]

The woman stood up, revolving on her heels as if she were propelled by a motor, and fell into convulsions. We felt pity for her. She was under the influence of perverse entities of darkness. She suffered mostly due to one such entity that attached to her. He appeared interested in ending her existence.

---

[14]**N.T.:** Spiritual Obsession is the dominance that some Spirits exercise over certain people. There exist three categories of those being spiritually obsessed: Simple, Fascination and Subjugation. Fascination comes in the form of an illusion produced by the direct action of a Spirit over the thoughts of the person. In this situation the person does not believe he or she is being deceived. This category of obsessor artfully inspires the person with blind confidence, which prevents him or her seeing the absurdity of his or her actions.

With a wolf-like howl, the unfortunate woman shouted and stomped on the floor. Raul watched with concerned distress and silently pleaded for divine mercy. Crawling snake-like, she acquired an animalistic look, even though she remained under the generous guard of the protectors of the Center.

Using advanced magnetic resources, Aulus and brother Clementino forced the obsessing Spirit to disassociate himself from the patient. She was still under his control, however, and he stayed close to her.

Our instructor lifted the injured one and sat her by her husband's side, explaining:

"It is a complex problem of fascination. Our sister is under the hypnotic control of an evil discarnate. Various companions assist him, allowing their desire for vengeance to defeat them. With their energy and hatred, he leaps over the poor soul and humiliates her by means of suggestion. Were it not for the fraternal resource from the sanctuary of prayer, she would have transformed into a victim of a deforming lycanthropy.[15] "Many perverted Spirits abuse the powers of intelligence, causing a feline cruelty over those who are still tied to them by past debts. Under intense hypnotic

---

[15]**N.T.:** Lycanthropy: The transformation of a human being into an animal. The term is derived from the Greek words, *lukos* a wolf, and *anthropos* a man, but it is employed regarding a transformation into any animal shape. (Lewis Spence, *"The Encyclopedia of the Occult,"* page 255). In Spiritism this is the state in which certain Spirits may find themselves in the spiritual world due to their inferiority or the hypnotic influence received from an evil Spirit.

action of such vampires, numerous patients imitate the costumes, positions and attitudes of diverse animals. This is the cause for many painful pictures that we see in the hospices."

As the patient groaned in a strange manner, her husband and Raul assist her. Hilario asked with astonishment: "Is such a painful phenomenon common?"

"It is common in the expiatory processes in which Spirits, related by their complicity in delinquency, fall into the vibratory planes of evildoers," Aulus explained, while helping to assist the patient. The victim's mind was controlled by the obstinate persecutor as a toy in a child's hand.

"And why not separate the executioner from his victim once and for all?"

"Be calm, Hilario" – said the mentor. "We have not yet examined the case intimately. Every obsession is founded on reciprocity. Let us recall the teaching of our divine Master. It is not enough to separate the wheat from the chaff; it is necessary to know how deep the roots penetrate the ground and how tightly they wrap around the wheat, so that we do not eradicate them both. There is no pain without justification. Therefore, let us collaborate with the Law of solidarity, without unknowingly anticipating the Divine justice."

Raul, under the direction of Clementino, tried to pacify the agitated communicant. He reminded him of the advantages of pardoning and tried to persuade him of the importance of humility and prayer. Not desiring to miss out on the lesson, my colleague approached Aulus, in anguish and said:

"But is verbal assistance enough to help those desperate brothers?"

"We will not offer them mere words, but more importantly our sentiments. Every word spoken with love is a projection of our self. Since we cannot offer them immediate relief, we give them instead our good will with words born in our hearts. We, as well, require Christ's redemption."

In an extremely significant tone, Aulus added: "We are all tied with bitter regrets to our past. This allows us to see that we need the same kind of assistance as the patients. We cannot speak for or against anyone because we all possess minor or greater debts to redeem."

Interrupting the conversation, our mentor calmed the executioner and the victim, who fought desperately. With fraternal care he showed that the patient and the pursuer equally deserved our affection.

Aulus applied passes to clear the patient's throat. A short time later, the executioner commenced to speak through her in an unintelligible manner. Through the thought wave that characterized the manifestation we could, however, discern the hatred that poured from his soul.

At the same time, Raul Silva heard the raised inflection of the entity's voice and attempted to calm him, but with little effect. As we demonstrated a mute question, Aulus observed the patient's face completely transfigured. He delayed a few minutes to observe the brain of the communicant as well as that of the medium, as if inquiring into the intimate world of each. After that, he returned to us.

Before the profound apprehension that Aulus' face expressed, Hilario took the initiative, inquiring in amazement, "To what can we attribute such a conflict?"

"I have penetrated the past to find out," responded the mentor sadly. "The roots of discord come from the distant past. Owing to our duty of not relating minor detail, which would give greater room for evil, I could say that their problem has existed for over a millennium.

"Our unfortunate brother speaks a dialect of ancient Tuscany where, while satisfying today's obsessed woman, he became a cruel strangler. He was a legionnaire of the powerful Duke Hugo of Provence of the 10th century. His present state shows the horrible reminiscences that torture him. He remembers the plundering in which he took part. To satisfy the woman who did not return his love, he killed his own parents. His heart overflows with bile."

As the mentor interrupted his tale, my colleague, naturally as interested as I was in knowing more, asked him for a more details of the past. Aulus, however, recommended that we limited our desire to investigate. No good would come of recalling horrific scenes in which these suffering souls engaged. They were two desperate hearts united in a hell of their own design. It would not be useful to peer into the fire and mud of their past.

Returning attention to our study, I questioned the language used. We were in Brazil and the obsessed sister used an obsolete dialect unfamiliar to us.

"Why, upon receiving the Spirit's thoughts through the uncontrollable wave lengths of his brain, did she not transform the words into modern Portuguese, as in numerous other processes of mediumistic communication we have observed?"

"We are in the presence of a case of polyglot mediumship, also called *xenoglossy*,"[16] explained the mentor. "The mediumistic filter and the Spirit that uses it are so closely knit that the instrument is under the absolute control of the will that directs it. Though strange to our ears, the obsessor's habits are those that regulated his existence centuries ago. Expressing himself through the medium, he makes use of phrases familiar to him."

---

[16]**N.T.: Xenoglossy:** The ability to speak or write in a language that has not been learned in the current incarnation.

"Is this attributable to mediumship or to the synchronization that existed between the two?" asked Hilario.

"It is a matter of synchronization," replied the mentor.

"Would the communicant be able to express himself in dialect if the medium had not spoken it in a prior incarnation?"

"Positively not!" exclaimed Aulus. "In all cases of xenoglossy, it is important to remember that forces of the past are carried over to the present. Discarnates, producing this kind of phenomenon interfere almost always through automatic impulses, in subconscious energies, but only do that through personalities with which they have had affinity.

"When an uneducated medium begins to write under the influence of a friend from our plane, the spiritual messenger does not miraculously remove the stones of ignorance. The psychographic medium brings in his or her memory from previous incarnations the art of writing and the discarnate companion manipulates it."

Hilario made the inquiring gesture of the apprentice and insisted, "We can then conclude that if the patient were a medium without ties to her past, the Spirit could not manifest through her with cultural characteristics foreign to her."

"Without a doubt," agreed the mentor. "In mediumship, synchronization also exists through time."

And with a bland countenance, he stressed:

"What we are witnessing can be to some degree compared to the currents of water. Each one holds its own particular level. The waters at sea level are useful and hold their peculiar enchantment. Yet only when cultured treasures surface from deep waters can their enormous latent force be used."

The lesson was of great value, but now we had to return to work. Through harmonized efforts, we had separated the executioner from the victim. According to our mentor, however, they were still united by distant magnetic ties.

Companions from our sphere removed the obsessing Spirit and lead him to a special rescue organization. In spite of this, the patient screamed, declaring that the horrible strangler was about to suffocate her.

Applying comforting passes, Aulus said, "This is solely a hallucinating phenomenon, which is typical with cases of fascination. The persecutor and the persecuted remain extremely close telepathically, acting and reacting mentally to each other."

Gradually, the patient became quiet. Once the crisis was over I asked Aulus what was the remedy for such a painful situation. He replied gravely:

"We are preparing the patient with an eye on resolving this case. She and the executioner will soon be mother and son; there is no other alternative for their redemption. As a woman, divine love will vibrate intensely in her and our sister will receive him to her breast.

Leaving us pensive, he immediately approached another person needing assistance and declared: "God be praised for the glory of the home!"

24

The Atoning Struggle

Near us, a gentleman seated among the patients went into trembling convulsions. If it had not been for the large easy chair in which he was seated, he would have been tossed to the ground. He was groaning and grunting in anguish as if an invisible hand were squeezing his throat.

Not far from him, two disagreeable looking Spirits were observing his movements and, without obviously employing magnetic action, provoked his agitation. The patient appeared physically mature but Aulus, quite moved, informed us:

"He is a poor brother who is going through an atoning struggle and who, in reality, has barely reached the age of thirty. From infancy, he suffered indirect influence from inferior companions of the past with whom he behaved badly. He was connected to these now discarnate Spirits for a long time prior to this reincarnation. When he senses their presence, he reflects on their evil influence that causes him hysterical disorders and weakens his desire for living.

"It has been an excruciating problem in the home to which he was reborn. From childhood, he has been to many doctors. Recently, he has undergone several medical treatments, such as Malaria therapy, insulin, and electroshock therapy, without any practical results. The painful and complex treatments took its toll on his body. He appears elderly when he should be vigorous and young."

While the pale patient trembled, Aulus and Clementino applied magnetic assistance, successfully calming his agitated body. Once the disturbing incident had passed, we noticed that he was sweating and forgetful, seemingly impervious to Raul Silva's prayers for Divine assistance on his behalf. After a few minutes, tranquility was completely restored.

The meeting was nearing its end; however the young man was apathetic and melancholic. Except for him, we observed that hope in varying degrees animated those present. Aulus, with his habitual tolerance, gave us his undivided attention.

"How are we to interpret this young man's condition?" asked Hilario with curiosity. "We did not see him out of his body. He did not also appear to assimilate a Spirit's fluidic emission. Could this be a mediumistic process unknown to us?"

"Our brother's illness," clarified the mentor, "is of a mental nature, but stems from his psychic sensitivity as in a mediumistic occurrence."

"If that is so," I added, "can we consider him a medium?"

"Not yet. Actually, at this time, he is a patient requiring careful assistance. Once this disharmony is corrected, he will be able to cultivate precious mediumistic faculties. Illness in this case is an important factor in storing valuable experience. Pain in our intimate life is similar to plowing undeveloped land: clawing and digging produces the best yield."

"And what is the origin of the sickness itself? Is it in the physical body or in the soul?" asked my companion with interest.

"It is the imbalanced state of the soul reflected in his physical body," replied the mentor moved. And caressing the forehead of the sad young man, he continued:

"Our friend, who is compensating for debts incurred prior to his reincarnation, wandered for many years in desolate darkness. There he was the victim of cruel hypnotizers. Due to the delinquent and corrupt activities in which he had been engaged in the world, he was in very close harmony with them. He suffered intensely and returned to Earth bringing with him deficiencies in his perispirit.

"He is a hysterical person. A heroic motherly heart received him but his father was his accomplice in evil activities. Today he also suffers while trying to achieve his recuperation. When he was seven, he started feeling the barrage of disharmony that he had brought from the spiritual world. He struggled with a laborious and self-imposed regenerative process ever since.

"Completely controlled by the disturbances that torture him, he supposes that he was born with congenital failure. He feels incapable of noble service and feels defeated even before he starts. He is only content with solitude, in which he nurtures sickly thoughts transmitted to his soul by his former companions. His nervous system is in a deplorable pathological state, characterized by strange disturbances of his intelligence that temporarily inhibits productive work."

The final prayer commenced, inviting us to observe silence. After the meeting ended Aulus offered to accompany the young patient home and Clementino approved. The young man was sleepy and drowsy, as if anesthetized. We assisted him through the streets for half an hour until we arrived at a simple suburban home. The young man called repeatedly before a lovely elderly lady answered.

"Americo, my son, thank God you are back."

Maternal tenderness vibrated in that clear and comforting voice. His mother took him inside. There was a young drunkard cursing. Looking at him she said quite preoccupied:

"Unfortunately, Marcio has once again indulged to excess." She looked at Americo and said: "But let me take care of you first."

The young man did not oppose. He accepted his mother's warm invitation and got under the bed sheets. Americo immediately went to sleep and appeared to us via a natural out-of-body experience. He was unaware of our presence, however, noticing only the mental disturbance that possessed him. In fear, he cautiously advanced through the small bedroom a short distance and tearfully threw himself upon an elderly paralytic, saying:

"Father, I am alone, alone! Who is going to rescue me? I am fearful, fearful!"

The elderly man, attentive and serene, sensed Américo's presence. His face had a painful expression as if he were hearing his son's complaints. Aulus suggested that I observe the patient's forehead as he lay on the clean cot. Trying to synchronize with him, I overheard him silently talking to himself:

"Oh Lord, I feel surrounded by uneasy Spirits. Who could it be that is close to me? Please, give me the strength to comprehend your wishes and accept your designs. Do not abandon me! Old age, illness and poverty are sad when we approach death."

And under the influence of the young man whose thoughts he unconsciously assimilated, he turned his head and started to cry inconsolably. Looking at them in a significant manner, our mentor explained to us:

"We are in the presence of Julio and his son Americo. Julio's legs are paralyzed and he has lived his entire life confined to his bed. Although bed-ridden, he sustains his family through manual labor. Given to loneliness and suffering, he made it a habit to read and reflect deeply. He learned the truth about reincarnation and received consolation and hope in the teachings of Spiritism. Because of this, he knows how to endure his trials with resignation and fortitude."

Aware of our thirst for more information, the mentor continued:

"Sustained by heroic solidarity with his wife, he brought five children into the world. One was a young girl who had been his dear sister in a prior life, and four youngsters, including Americo. The parents found it difficult to care and guide for these four. Marcio, who we already know, has a proclivity to drunkenness. William and Benicio are wasting their youth in nightlife. Laura is the devoted companion of her parents, and Americo, the first born, still cannot recuperate his own equilibrium."

Observing the head of the household in such a situation, Hilario interrupted: "We can only imagine the difficulty in that house."

"Without a doubt, the expiation of this family is painful and difficult. In the not too distant past, Julio was the head of a small band of evildoers. Extremely ambitious and dedicated to robbery and gangs, he attacked innocent travelers. He was able to convince four of his friends to accompany him in the lustful adventures that dominated him, thus compromising their moral lives.

"These four former companions are the sons who are in his care today and cause him worry and despair. He once led them to veer from the righteous path and now is trying to reinstate them toward a dignified life. At the same time, he finds himself trying to withstand sorrowful inhibitions."

We were moved by the elderly man's resignation. However, new circumstances called our attention. A noble and serene young lady entered the room in spirit form and passed us unaware of our presence. Reassuring Americo, she took him outside.

Perceiving our curiosity, the assistant clarified: "It is Laura, the generous daughter, who even while physically asleep, does not neglect caring for her sick father."

"Does she live here?" asked my colleague with astonishment.

"Yes, she sleeps in the adjoining room."

After administering new vitality to the patient, who was overcome with tears, the mentor added: "When the physical body rests, the soul does not always do the same. In the majority of the cases, it continues with its own impulses. Whoever is dedicated to goodness works the land sown with seeds of love; anyone who is enmeshed in evil will continue to have nightmares that torture him."

"According to our analysis," said Hilario, "mediumistic deeds in the home are continuous."

"Exactly!" confirmed the mentor. "The thoughts of those who share the same roof interact in a particular way, using unceasing currents of assimilation. Incarnates influence each other in ways much greater than one could imagine. Many times the obsessors that trouble us reincarnate in our environment. In the same manner, there are protecting Spirits that assist us who also participate in our everyday experiences.

"It is vital to understand that we always and everywhere live in spirit. The interchange between parents and children, husbands and wives, brothers and sisters, friends and companions, affections and indifferences, in the family circuit or in the institutions of service in which we grouped ourselves, is obligatory and constant. We take advantage of the ideas and strength from one another without always being aware of it."

We were about to leave when Hilario, anxious for clarification, asked: "Returning to Americo's case, and since we recognize him to be hysterical, would it be of any advantage for him to frequent a group where there are other mediums who are also developing?"

"Of course," responded the mentor, "progress results from cooperation. By dedicating himself to discipline, study, meditation and prayer, he will renovate his mind and accelerate his own cure. He then will be able to cooperate in rewarding mediumistic tasks. Every dignified effort, no matter how small, invariably receives its best response from life."

After that, Aulus recalled that there were other tasks to accomplish and ended the current lesson.

25

Regarding Mental Fixation

On the way back, Hilario and I asked our mentor to teach us about mental fixation. On many occasions I had observed this phenomenon and tried to study it. Since Hilario was newer than I was in spiritual services, I raised the subject for his benefit.

My colleague, although preoccupied, and still frightened by the manifestation of the strangler of Tuscany, said:

"I try sincerely but I cannot resolve the enigmas posed by certain situations and emotions. How can the mind hold impressions and become paralyzed by them as if time did not pass? For instance, our unfortunate companion has remained transfixed for centuries with the desire for vengeance. Could he possibly have been in this lamentable situation for so many years without reincarnating?"

Aulus listened attentively and pondered:

"After the physical body's dies, we continue developing thoughts cultivated during our corporeal experience. Since universal principles are unavoidable, how can we progress without attaining harmony? The fixed idea stops mental life indefinitely."

"Let us symbolize the apprenticeship of the reincarnated soul as if it were a strategic battle position established for individual and collective perfection. If this were the case, the heart should arm itself with edifying ideas to achieve the great victory of inner purification. The mind is a soldier that battles successfully and is then conducted to death's door, rising toward the Superior Sphere, expressing triumph through the level of elevation it achieved.

"If it fails, it is usually the result of negligence or rebellion. In death, it returns to the inferior circuits where it mingles among the maladjusted and spends an indefinite period in treatment. In any earthly struggle, the rearguard is the tormented position of the neurotics, the crazed, the mutilated and the injured."

Aware of our interest, Aulus continued, "The victorious legions do not forget about those who remain unbalanced. Because of this, we witness diligent missions of love and renunciation wherever disharmony and pain exist."

"And what about the soul's stagnancy?" – asked my colleague, anxious for knowledge.

The mentor smiled and said: "Let me present you with an image so that we can define this with great assurance. As measured by a clock, an hour does not vary. This is not true, however, of the way we perceive that same hour. When we are happy we do not notice the minutes passing. The days fly by rapidly when we satisfy our ideals, desires and interests. When suffering or fearful, however, we have the impression that time is standing still.

"When we do not make an effort to overcome the slow pace of anguish, the afflicted or obsessive ideas ruin our mental life by transforming it into a fixed idea. As we begin to gravitate in spirit around this erroneous point, time appears crystallized within us. Whether we call an inner disturbance passion or disenchantment, cruelty or vengeance, jealousy or desperation, it can immobilize us indefinitely in its net of darkness. This results when we refuse to march incessantly with the Supreme good.

"Let us also analyze our symbol of combat. The inflexible clock indicates the same time for everyone; however, time weighs lightly for those who triumphed and heavy for those who failed. For the triumphant, the days are happy and honorable; for the vanquished, they are anguished and tearful. To liberate ourselves from the thoughts that beat and depress us, we need to renew ourselves. Without this, we are transformed into disheartened phantoms of affliction, being mutilated in our highest hopes or trapped in our intimate sores.

"When death surprises us under these conditions, our experience is aggravated if the Spirit is not disposed to the heroic effort of supreme renunciation. It may easily be tangled up in fixations that cause it to relive unhappy reminiscences for years or even centuries. Absorbed only by one's pain, laziness or hatred, the discarnate person appears like an animal that remains in a lethargic dream of hibernation. The Spirit separates itself from the outside world, vibrating around the hidden unbalance that makes it satisfied. It hears, sees and feels nothing else outside of the delirious idea that preoccupies it."

The subject matter was of immense personal interest to me. On many occasions I had observed first-hand that certain consciences were asleep after death and appeared as spiritual mummies. I reminded Aulus of this.

He appreciated the question: "Yes, the stationary mind, because it violates the Law, goes through anguishing nightmares during its habitual state of hibernation after death, and when it awakens it finds itself in a state of alienation. This can persist for a long time if it passionately cultivates the impressions in which it believes it finds happiness."

"And what is the remedy in this situation?" – I respectfully inquired.

"In time, many of those disoriented souls will finally tire of evil and seek their personal regeneration. Others awaken with our assistance to the responsibilities needed for personal readjustment. They are like wounded soldiers that try to respond to the missions of love, which assist them with their recovery. They understand the importance of the dignifying struggle, assisting whoever helps them and returning to combat, where they discover how to serve goodness.

"On the other hand, souls that are obstinate rebels are kindly obliged to return to the battle in order to abandon the state of discouragement they chose to live in. The experience in a corporeal body acquired during difficult situations is similar to an intense combat in which the soul can recuperate. For this, the interested party relies on the affectionate attention of family members."

"In those cases, is reincarnation necessary even if it violates the person's free will?"

"What do we do on Earth when an insane person enters our home? Don't we assume responsibility for how we treat the person? Would we wait for a remedy from the person before we choose how best to restore his ou her equilibrium?

"We should honor a free conscience capable of responding to various problems it encounters while evolving. An irresponsible and ill patient, however, needs our fraternal collaboration, even if regaining their equilibrium is a painful process."

And after a brief pause, Aulus continued: "Reincarnation in such circumstances is equivalent to placing an inert patient in a friction-producing machine that awakens him through its movements. The soul, in an intimate juxtaposition with the cells, is a happy prisoner of the physical body, in which it influences the atomic world as much as it is influenced by it, and works through the necessary difficulties for its recuperation."

These significant observations invited us to meditate and learn. Quite impressed, I said: "Similar fixations is one reason that we see so many Spirits affected by a deplorable amnesia. When they communicate with the incarnate brothers and sisters, they don't have a clear and general recall except for the matters retained in their preoccupied memory. And then, when they exchange impressions with us, they appear as chronic psychotics."

"Exactly. And it is for this reason that they have to be treated with loving warmth."

"When these souls are on their way toward reincarnation and they face the difficulties born of their errors, do they immediately understand their reality?" I asked with enthusiasm.

"No, not always."

Changing the tone of his voice, the mentor continued:

"In the majority of the cases, progress is slow. We can prove this through the study of retarded youngsters, an affliction that is a painful enigma. Only by supreme love from the parents and family members can the essential infusion of warmth and vitality be administered to those small children, who frequently remain for many years in the material world. They can be viewed as tortured appendixes of terrestrial society. Although their suffering might appear unjustifiable, it serves as a necessary and effective remedy. We can also observe this truth in the schizophrenic or paranoid. They have lost their sense of proportion and thus have an erroneous concept of themselves.

"Almost all of the congenital disturbances of the mind, which manifest upon the reincarnation, reflect fixed ideas that existed prior to the return to Earth. In many cases, the incarnate Spirits live, from cradle to grave, in a gradual process of recovery through beneficial struggles. Human therapeutics and domestic obligations, as well as impositions of customs and social conflicts, give them the cure for the psychosis they suffer, because they work as a process of awakening for the soul."

The conversation was instructive and suggested other important studies to us. Our mentor, however, still had other services to perform.

26

Psychometry[17]

Our lessons were coming to a close. Since Aulus had many commitments, he did not have time to give us further demonstrations. Although Hilario and I understood it, we felt somewhat melancholy. Aulus, however, found every way to keep us from losing our enthusiasm.

---

[17]**N.T.:** Psychometry: A term used by spiritualists to denote the faculty of reading the characters, surroundings, etc., of persons, by holding in the hand small objects, such as a watch or ring, which they have had in their possession. The honor of having discovered the psychometric faculty belongs to Dr. J. R. Buchanan, who classed it among the sciences, and gave it the name it bears. (Lewis Spence, *"The Encyclopedia of the Occult,"* page 333).

We crossed streets and plazas and finally stopped in front of a museum. Some last minute visitors were entering. Aulus, inclined to take advantage of the time that we had left to make a few observations, invited us to enter.

He said: "In an institution such as this, very interesting studies are possible. Surely you have heard about psychometry. As used in experimental psychology, it means "registration, appreciation of intellectual activity." In mediumship, this word defines the faculty of perceiving impressions and memories from ordinary objects."

We entered through a wide doorway. Inside there were many discarnate entities and people admiring useful articles of times gone by.

"Many companions who fixate on the past often come to places such as this for the simple pleasure of recalling the past," commented the mentor.

The precious objects there, except for one or two, had an opaque energy that formed a grayish mass out of which some luminous points were observed. Noticing my curiosity, the mentor benevolently clarified:

"All the objects you see penetrated by fluidic substances are often remembered and visited by those who possessed them."

Not too far away there was a curious clock circled by a luminous whitish band. Aulus recommended that I touch it. Almost instantly, in my mind's eye, a lovely family appeared. A venerable couple enjoyed a conversation with four young men in the prime of their lives.

In that living mental picture, I observed the room was pleasant and dignified. The Austrian furniture denoted sobriety and nobility, which was further beautified by large flowered vases and valuable paintings. The clock was there, dominating from on top of an old capriciously adorned wall.

Observing my surprise, the mentor continued: "I can perceive the images without touching it directly. The clock belonged to a respectable family of the 19th century. It holds the thoughts of the couple that acquired it and who periodically feel happy visiting the museum to recollect. The reminiscences of the former owners, memories relived through time, animate the clock through spiritual ties of the affectionate circle they left behind."

Hilario touched the precious piece and said: "That means that we see images impregnated by their vibrations."

"Exactly," confirmed the mentor. "The clock is surrounded by mental currents of the brothers who are still attached to it, similar to the way a copper wire conducts energy sensitized by electric current. Observing its state, we immediately relate to the memories of those who hold it in high regard."

Hilario reflected for a few moments and observed: "Therefore, if we were interested in meeting those companions, this kind of object could serve as a mediator?"

"Yes, exactly," approved the mentor, "we could use an object in which their thoughts are concentrated. Anything that radiates from our thoughts facilitates these connections."

"The analysis of mental forces is very important in this study," I mused, completely dominated by a strong impression.

Aulus smiled and added: "Our thoughts spread our personal emanations toward every area into which they are projected. An animal leaves traces of his own characteristic odor, and for that reason dogs can easily recognize it. We leave spiritual vestiges wherever we project the effluvium of our mind. When we are free from our physical body, our senses become more acute and we can perceive without difficulty phenomena that our spiritual evolvement permits."

"We are induced to believe," considered my companion, "that we don't have the resources to register the thoughts of those more evolved than we are."

"Yes, those who have reached an elevation that we cannot even imagine belong to higher planes, rising above our manner of being and expression. Their thoughts vibrate in another frequency. Naturally, they can accompany and assist us, because it is the Law that superior souls reach inferior ones when they wish. However, we are not able to do the same."

Aulus reflected an instant and continued: "A comparison will help us to understand better. What occurs between them and us also occurs between us and souls less advanced than us. For example, we can help primitive tribes but they cannot do the same for us.

"Through study we know the customs and have other knowledge about tribal men or women, but it is impossible for them to understand the culture of our society. Thought conditions us to the circle in which we should or deserve to live. Only through our own efforts or through a solid evolvement are we able to perfect thought, thereby overcoming its limitations and causing it to vibrate in superior spheres."

Aulus looked at us with kindness and added: "Meanwhile, let us not digress."

"Let us imagine," I said, "that we make a more minute examination. Could we look into the history of the material that comprises this clock?"

"Without a doubt. This would require more work and more time; notwithstanding, it is a perfectly viable initiative."

"Each object then," concluded Hilario, "can be both a mediator for people interested in it and a registry of nature's records."

"Exactly" confirmed Aulus, sounding confident. "The paleontologist is able to reconstitute pieces of pre-historic fauna from a simple bone. When our sensibility is more intense and purified, we will be able to observe in simple abandoned objects vibrations that express characteristics of the people that possessed them or the events that they witnessed."

Then, smiling, he added: "Souls and objects, each one in its corresponding place, preserve some part of time and space which are eternal in the memory of life."

Later we stopped to admire a beautiful painting from the 18th century, which did not appear to have any fluidic vestige. It was, in effect, an isolated beauty and we couldn't establish spiritual contact with it.

Aulus assumed, as usual, the attitude of benevolent professor, and explained: "Investigated deeply, this painting could be an interesting recording that offers us certain data of its elements. Meanwhile, it is not a mediator of spiritual relationships, for it seems to have been completely forgotten by the author and those that possessed it."

We continued to a large gallery where two gentlemen and three ladies were admiring a mirror. Nearby, a young discarnate woman displayed great sadness. One of the ladies made a remark regarding the beauty of the mirror's frame. Immediately, the young girl manifested as an irritated guard and touched the onlooker's shoulders.

The woman shivered involuntarily and told her companions: "I have a strange feeling that we are in a funeral chamber. It would be better if we left."

The group made some good-humored remarks over what had been said and left for another exhibition hall. The Spirit, who had not noticed our presence, appeared content in her solitude. She contemplated the mirror as if she were under a strong spell.

Aulus soothed her gently as he touched the object, and commented: "Did you observe the phenomenon? Of the small group of visitors, the sister who felt the closeness of the young woman possesses a great mediumistic sensitivity. If she educated these forces and scrutinized the mirror, she would enter into an immediate relationship with the discarnate lady. She would receive her confidences and learn her intimate drama. She would immediately assimilate her mental wavelength and thus capture the images."

Hilario, incapable of controlling his curiosity, asked about the young lady: "What was she doing there in a graveyard of remembrances? Why is she so interested in a simple mirror of seemingly little significance?"

Aulus, as if expecting our question, answered without hesitation: "I touched the object and saw that a young man gave this original mirror to this girl he promised to marry. I can see his romantic figure in his thoughts of her.

"He was the son of a French couple who took refuge in Brazil during the French Revolution in 1791. At that time, he was a boy. His family moved to Rio de Janeiro and there he grew to manhood. He met this girl and conquered her heart. United by an intimate affection, they planned their marriage. Happy over the successes of Napoleon in Europe, however, the exiled family decided to return to their country.

"The young man was desolated but obeyed the paternal decision. He said farewell to his fiancée and asked her to save the mirror as a remembrance until he could come back. When it happens, they would be happy forever. In France, however, he fell in love with another woman and never returned. He quickly forgot his responsibilities and compromise, becoming indifferent to his former love.

"The poor young girl remained true to her promise and waited for him. The mirror is the jewel of her happiness. I can imagine the long journey that she made through the course of time, caring for it as her special property until it found its way to this museum."

"This is reminiscent," I said, "of ancient tales about bewitched jewels."

"Yes, yes," pondered the mentor, "the influence does not originate from the jewels but rather from the forces that accompany them."

Hilario, who was intently meditating on the lesson, said: "What would happen if someone acquired the object?"

"Surely," interrupted the mentor, "he would also sense the presence of the discarnate young woman."

"Would that be just?"

Aulus smiled and said: "Hilario, life never makes mistakes. It is possible that someone could appear here, fall in love with the object and dispute its possession."

"Who?"

"The young man who made the promise and provoked her mental fixation on the object, or the woman for whom he broke his promise. Being both of them reincarnate, in the present or in the future, it is possible that they come here and may attract her to them, so that she may be their daughter or their companion. Therefore, they would pay off the debt that they incurred.

"But couldn't a circle of cure liberate the discarnate girl from the disturbances that victimize her?"

"Yes," asserted the mentor, "this is also possible. Nevertheless, examining the harmonious operation of the Law, it is inevitable that the three will reunite. The problems we create we must also resolve."

The conversation was truly a lesson; however, our responsibilities propelled us forward. We passed by the administrative office of the museum. Seeing two empty chairs close to a small worktable, my colleague asked a question hoping to complete the lesson:

"I believe that the auxiliaries of the museum's administration use these chairs. If we sat in them, would we be able to relate to their usual occupants?"

"Yes, if we desired," assured the mentor.

"And what about the incarnates?" continued Hilario. "If a person receives clothes, beds, adornments, or other objects that belong to others, will he or she feel the effluvia of those that used them?"

"Perfectly well. To register them, however, they need an acute psychic sensitivity. We provoke goodness or evil in those that come in contact with us through vibrations that originate in the characteristics of our individuality."

"Is all we have witnessed here mediumship?"

"Yes, despite the experimenters of the scientific world who categorize them as *pragmatic criptestesia*, *metagnomia* tactile, *telestesia*, etc.

Leading the way toward the public thoroughfare, he concluded: "There is perception, affinity and synchronization everywhere, and this points to one truth: through our thoughts, we commune with one another in the heart of Universal life."

27

Misguided Mediumship

Nightfall had come when we entered a narrow room where a group of people was praying. We saw various entities in a lamentable condition amidst the incarnates. Their appearance was inferior to the men and women that participated in the reunion.

Aulus introduced us to Cassio, an amiable protective Spirit, and the only one there that appeared to be morally superior. His spiritual isolation was evidenced by the fact that the discarnates and incarnates of the assembly could not perceive his presence, or be aware of his thoughts. Though discouraged, Cassio manifested in answer to our mentor's appeals:

"So far no progress has been made, even though we made repeated calls for a renovation. We surrounded Quintino with the best resources, putting books and articles at his reach and generating uplifting conversations, but all in vain. Our friend is not yet aware of the great responsibilities that he assumes as head of a group of this kind."

Aulus tried to comfort him with a silent but understanding gesture. We were invited to observe.

The room was filled with dense, disagreeable fluids. Two mediums communicated with some companions from our plane. My first impression was that they were paid as the group's servants for undignified services. Diverse entities in the same condition, servile and meddlesome, formed a crowd around them.

Trance communication was common there. The mediums, out of their bodies, fed on the peculiar emanations of those present.

Raimundo, one of the communicating Spirits, under the kind eye of the director of the Center, conversed with a lady whose indiscretions and impudence inspired pity.

"Raimundo," she said, "I need money. For months the Institute that owes me has not paid me. What do you say with regard to the delay?"

"Wait, dear sister," recommended the entity, "we will act in your behalf."

The conversation continued: "My situation requires urgent solution. You should be more forceful. Go to the office of the director and eliminate the difficulties. Do you want the addresses of the people you need to influence?"

"No, no! I know them and where they live."

"I noticed, Raimundo, that you are distracted. You are not working promptly on my behalf."

"That is not true. I have done as much as I can."

And, while the lady lowered her voice and chatted, a mature gentleman directed his attention to Teotonio, the other communicating Spirit, declaring calmly: "Teotonio, how long should I wait?"

He appeared surprised by the question. He was silent and humble but the questioner added firmly: "I have been waiting four months to get the job that was promised to me. Couldn't you solve my problem?"

"What would you like me to do?"

"I know that the manager of the company is against me. Influence him and make him give me a job."

In the meantime, another lady also solicited Raimundo's attention.

"Dear friend, I am relying on your valuable assistance. My daughter has accepted a marriage proposal from a shameless individual. This has created an alarming situation at home. My husband cannot stand this man and our daughter's annoyance torments us. Couldn't you do something to get him away from our home?"

Raimundo answered, respectfully, while Quintino immediately called for a prayer, so that the discarnates could increase their forces in order to respond to the group's trust and reply to the services solicited. The arrangements and conversations continued between those communicating and the clients of the house, but I did not pay any further attention, considering all of this to be trivial.

I've seen obsessors and entities involved in evil doings under afflictive circumstances and enmeshed in tremendous conflicts, but nowhere did I feel so much compassion as I felt there. Here were healthy and clear-headed people communicating with the spiritual world as if it were a system for criminal exploitation and based on the principle of least effort.

Could those men and women have the impudence to request from incarnate companions the kind of services they were requesting from Spirits? Aren't they abusing prayer and mediumship to escape the problems that surrounded them? Don't they have enough knowledge to use their brain, tongue, eyes, ears, hands and feet in ennobling lessons? What were they doing with their faith? Could we justify a worker who turns over his or her share of work to others for the world's improvement?

Aulus detected my bitter reflections and kindly hurried to comfort me.

"Any study of mediumship, even one as quick as ours, would not be complete if we did not investigate the misguided psychic region in which lazy Spirits, incarnates and discarnates, feed off each other. This is a product of ignorance that exists in churches throughout the world. They abuse prayer as much as they despise the opportunities that dignified work gives. They search for undeserved favors and transitory advantages, thus giving into indolence that crystallizes their childish wishes."

"Will they continue this way indefinitely?" I asked.

"Andre, your question surprises me. You possess enough experience to know that pain is the great minister of Divine justice. Our lives are a great battle of evolvement. Whoever flees from the sacrificial task now encounters pain later. The Spirit may feel confident in inactivity, criminally mobilizing the will. One day, however, his torment will arrive and force him to understand the imperatives of progress. You can't flee from eternity because time, the benefactor of work, is also the executioner of inertia."

Hilario, who reflected nearby in silence and preoccupation, asked:

"Why do our incarnate brothers lend themselves to such practices in which little effort is required of them? There are so many lessons for spiritual improvement and so many calls for dignified mediumship in the doctrinal directives of Spiritism! Why is there so much disequilibrium?

Aulus thought a moment and answered.

"Hilario, what we see here is not what the Spiritist Doctrine prescribes. We are witnessing the mediumistic phenomena managed by idle minds, which are attracted by inferior exploitation and thus worthy of our great pity. We cannot ignore that the mediumistic phenomenon involves people and churches everywhere. On the other hand, it is understandable that our friends, while on Earth, prefer to communicate with discarnates who remain bound to the sensorial field of physical life without a wider vision of the realities of the Spirit.

"It is easier for the common individual to work with equals or subordinates, since working with superiors requires goodwill, discipline, a timely correction of their actions, and a firm desire to improve.

"We know that there are no miracles at death. Each person awakens beyond the grave in the spiritual situation that he or she created. The vulgar individual feels better with entities that flatter his passions and stimulate his or her appetites. This is because, when we are before evolved companions, who have already learned to sublimate their personal impulses, dedicating themselves incessantly to goodness, we feel obliged to educate ourselves."

"But isn't this an abuse of the incarnate individual? Isn't it a crime for him to take advantage of inferior discarnates?" asked Hilario.

"Without a doubt," confirmed Aulus.

"Does this crime remain unpunished?"

Aulus observed with a good humored expression and responded:

"Don't be too preoccupied. When errors originate from well-intentioned ignorance, the Law provides the necessary resources to enlightenment because genuine charity, in any circumstance, is always venerable. If the abuse is deliberate, however, punishment is inevitable."

He directed his glance at the director of the reunion and to the intermediaries of the communicating mediums, and added:

"Teotonio, Raimundo and discarnate Spirits like them are in reality not the ones who take control but the ones controlled. Fascinated by Quintino's requirements and the mediums that collaborate in such an unfortunate venture, they are apprentices who continue in their mentor's path.

"If the director and the mediums in this group do not dedicate themselves to goodness, the Spirits that their work has enslaved will surprise them when they discarnate, asking for orientation and help. Probably later, in another epoch, all of them, the victims, will be reunited in the same family on Earth as parents and children. By correcting their attitudes, they shall achieve the complete liberation of their debts."

With our silent admiration, the mentor concluded: "Each noble deed receives the payment due to it, and each unhappy venture pays its price."

Aulus, then, invited us to depart. The atmosphere did not lend itself to further study and we had already learned there the lesson that we could receive.

28

Physica Effects Phenomena

It was 8:00 pm when we entered a small apartment where a mediumship meeting of materialization was about to begin. Hilario and I did not want to conclude our week of study without observing this kind of phenomenon in the company of the mentor.

On another occasion we witnessed materialization and outlined our impressions.[18] Nonetheless, Aulus' teachings had a moral foundation that made them

---

[18]"Missionaries of the Light" – (note of the Spiritual Author)

valuable and informative. The thought of listening to him discuss this physical phenomenon made me happy.

The place designated for the work consisted of two linked rooms: a living room and a narrow bedroom. The latter room, transformed into a consulting room, was designated for a young man who was a medium. In the living room, fourteen apparently well-intentioned individuals were gathered. From this group, two sick ladies stood out. They were the principal motive for this reunion, since they sought friendly assistance from the materialized Spirits.

Pointing to them, the mentor spoke seriously: "Bear in mind that I accompany you here to aid the sick. Although many attempts of materialization of forces from our plane have been done on Earth, in general they are based in the negative attitudes of our incarnate brothers. According to our view, only the sick justify efforts of this type, unless it is for dignified and respectable scientific work, which will benefit all mankind."

We wanted further clarification but various workers coming and going reminded us that the task for the evening was about to begin. These workers were cleaning the ambient, since the service requires great caution. Some used delicate instruments that emitted curative rays, while others ionized the environment with bacterial effects. Some incarnates often did not take the responsibility of their actions seriously. Their bodies exuded toxic emanations from nicotine abuse, the consumption of meat and aperitifs and thoughts that worked against the group's work.

Attentive to the study, we followed Aulus' recommendation to concentrate our attention on the medium's cabinet. Constant activity was taking place around him. Dozens of well-directed and disciplined Spirits were busy with preparatory activities. The medium had already received aid to his digestive, circulatory and visceral areas.

We will not discuss materialization's substances, associations, resources and movements on the spiritual plane, as those are discussed in another book.[19] We are interested now in analyzing mediumship and its behavior with regard to environment and people. For that, our dedicated and competent mentor was all we needed.

As was customary, the lights were turned off. An opening prayer was said and the group sang Evangelical Hymns to improve the vibrations in the room. Collaborating discarnates drew energies from persons and objects in the living room as well as from nature. These energies united to the elements from our sphere and transformed the mediumistic chamber into a beautiful and complex laboratory.

As a result of the magnetic actions employed by the responsible workers, the medium left his physical

---

[19] "Missionaries of the Light" – (note of the Spiritual Author)

body, which remained on the bed inert and abandoned. The separation was so perfect that it appeared to be an actual disincarnation.

The physical body lay prostrate and under the control of the technicians from our plane. It started to expel ectoplasm from every pore. It appeared as a flexible paste, similar to a glutinous jelly and semi-liquefied. It came out in great quantities through the natural orifices, particularly the mouth, nose and ears. In addition, a great amount was exteriorized through the thorax and extremities of the fingers.

The substance, characterized by an indefinable odor, was being expelled in a reptile-like movement. Accumulating on the lower area of the mediumistic body, it presented the aspect of a large protoplasmic mass, live and tremulous. Our companions gave endearing assistance to the medium as if he were a patient or a child.

Aulus clarified: "The ectoplasm is in itself closely associated with the mediums' thoughts, similar to the way a child during gestation is attached to the maternal mind. Because of this, we must proceed with great caution while assisting the medium."

Hearing this, Hilario asked: "Is this caution due to the possibility of an inconvenient intervention on the part of the medium?"

"Exactly."

Aulus continued: "If the medium were better educated we would not have to be as cautious or need to interfere, since he would collaborate with us. To materialize individuals and objects from our plane as perfectly as possible requires a safe dematerialization of the medium and the incarnate companions that assist him or her. As the delivery of pure water depends on the cleanliness of the channel through which it flows, we also depend on the cooperation of our earthly friends, in spite of putting our best efforts into this kind of work.

"That means," said my colleague, "that the mediumistic thought can influence materialized forms even when they are under the rigorous control of Spirit friends."

"Yes," confirmed the mentor. "Even when the medium cannot completely control them, one can interfere in their formation and projection, and jeopardize our services. That is why those dedicated to its achievements are willing to comply with the task as much as possible."

Hilario, although satisfied, continued pondering: "In this manner, the ability to materialize does not constitute a privilege to those who possess it."

"Under no circumstances." And after a brief pause he added: "The very word *materialization* embodies the truth of the subject. To materialize means "to become physical." The word *mediumship* does not imply sublimity but service. And, since death does not purify the impure, how could we attribute sanctity to the mediums on Earth, or to those who communicate through them, by the simple act of modeling passing forms between both planes?"

"Then, that strength..." My companion did not finish. Aulus perceived his thoughts and cut him short.

"That materialized force is similar to others used for interchange. It does not depend on the character or moral quality of those who possess it. It emanates from the psychophysical world, and cytoplasm is but one of its origins. In some rare individuals a larger percentage of this energy is externalized. In the future, when the human community achieves a more elevated degree of maturity, it will be more abundant and much easier to come across."

"Until then, there will be no way..."

"Until then, we will use these possibilities as someone might an unripe fruit in certain special circumstances. This person, however, shall undergo unpleasant surprises to pick it. Therefore, when we face this kind of experience, we shall tolerate certain undesirable mediumistic interferences, as well as some undignified influences of our companions incarnate, who are frankly inept for services of this nature.

Hilario, concentrating on the lesson, pondered: "Let us imagine that the medium has inferior inclinations, be it an uncontrolled affection, an unmeasured ambition, or a personal point of view that originate in common passions. Under these conditions, could he influence the phenomena that we are analyzing?"

"Without a doubt," answered Aulus calmly, "consciously or unconsciously."

"And what if the rest of the group were involved in unsavory purposes, could they interfere?"

"Most certainly!"

"Then, why should we associate with incapable elements?"

The mentor's eyes shone expressively and, tapping Hilario on the shoulder said with good sense: "Don't say *incapable elements*. Let us say *uninformed elements*. We need to accept imperfect or inefficiently practiced mediumship as if it were unclean water. We need it pure but use it in whatever condition we find it, if we are extremely thirsty. After that, we will patiently liberate the fountain, little by little, of its impurities.

"Mankind is developing sublime mediumship through dignified and conscientious mediums who follow the mandate to make mediumship something eternal and divine. This is not a task of precipitation. Improvisation cannot make a lasting foundation on which to construct sanctuaries of wisdom and of love."

My colleague and I smiled with satisfaction over that monumental manifestation of comprehension and tolerance. Meanwhile, a large milky-silvery mass of ectoplasm had formed, in which some dark and grayish threads could be seen. Technicians from our plane controlled it carefully.

Aulus explained the work: "There we have the light plastic material that is needed for the materialization. Briefly, we can divide it into three essential elements: *A* fluids, representing the superior and subtle forces from our sphere; *B* fluids, defining the resources of the medium and assisting companions; and *C* fluids, constituting energies taken from the Earth.

"*A* fluids can be considered the purest and *C* fluids the most docile; however, *B* fluids, born from the collaboration of the incarnate companions and particularly of the medium, are capable of destroying our noblest projects. In rare circles or groups where the *A* elements effectively find cooperation of the *B* energies, the materializations assume the highest characteristics, approaching the sublime due to the tenor of the phenomenon.

"However, wherever *B* elements predominate, our participation is considerably reduced because we must channel through inferior forces from our plane. They attune to the incarnate brothers and sisters and can dominate their resources, controlling their actions and leading their psychic experiences to lamentable disasters.

The elucidation could not be clearer. We were preparing to continue our study when Garcez, one of the spiritual technicians of the service, solicited magnetic assistance from Aulus.

The fluidic field in the room was heavy. The small projections of ectoplasm, thrown experimentally toward the adjoining room, returned to the cabinet with an elevated grade of toxins.

All fourteen people united in the room were capricious individuals. There was no one who understood the effort required by the spiritual world. Instead of helping the medium, each of them weighed him down with his or her absurd requests. For this reason, the medium did not have sufficient tranquility to act. He resembled a restless animal cornered by darts due to the negative thoughts he received.

"In this manner, we cannot achieve a materialization of a superior order." spoke the mentor, deep in thought.

"Surely, surely." Garcez informed us with disappointment. "We will only have the medium in an out-of-body experience and under the influence of our nurse, who will assist the ill sisters. Nothing more. We do not have the required concurrence."

Aulus responded to the request and magnetically assisted in the transfer of energies from the physical body to the perispiritual body. We immediately noticed a surge of animation. The physical body in the bed was prostrate but the medium, in his perispirit, had greater vitality and clarity. The spiritual friends engulfed him in a large ectoplasmic robe and the nurse joined him, directing his movements.

The medium, in spite of being absent from his corporeal body, was under the control of the benefactor. He was similar to a trance medium, except that his clothes were structured by ectoplasmic energy, which was crucial because it kept him in the room, in spite of the perturbed and unquiet thoughts that are reflected in the ambient.

Watching him walk unsteadily and accompanied by the nurse, Hilario murmured to our mentor: "Is the medium conscious during this phenomenon?"

"While he is out-of-body, but he might not recall it when he returns to the physical field."

Hilario ventured: "We see him with a materialized robe and orientated by the friendly nurse. If he had inappropriate desires under these conditions, could he jeopardize the task?"

"Exactly," said Aulus, "he is under control; however, control does not eliminate his will. Any improper impulse he has would affect the service. That is the problem when this type of activity is developed without an elevated moral objective.

The mediating therapist, guided by the generous Spirit, reached the narrow room. He wore a delicate robe, similar to a tunic of a lunar clarity that emitted a silvery light. As he crossed through the atmosphere of the room, its clarity lessened until it almost diminished completely.

To our questioning look the mentor responded: "The neural psychic state of the incarnate companions are not helpful. They absorb our resources without recuperating the fluids that have been laboriously created for them."

The mentor invited us into the living room. Dark mental emissions emerged, continuously and lamentably striking each other. Our incarnate friends acted as unconscious children. They had undesirable thoughts and made absurd requests in their apparent silence. They requested the presence of beloved discarnates, without regarding to the potential this opportunity offered, or to their own merit. Instead, they criticized, differing over particularities of the phenomenon, or filled their imaginations with dishonorable problems of earthly life.

They did not consider the spiritual friends' work as a kindness from benefactors, but rather as a useless spectacle created by worthless servants. In spite of that, workers from our plane offered their best efforts to the success of the task.

The delicate nurse applied curative rays to the patients. Occasionally, she left the room and then returned, because even the simplest inappropriate thought could jeopardize her vibrations. The ectoplasm darkened under the bombardment of the mental forms born of the reunion's assistants.

When the healing was over, a happy companion from our sphere picked up a small portion of the materialized forces of the medium and departed. A few seconds later, he returned and distributed flowers to the incarnate brothers with the intention of calming their excited minds.

Putting our curiosity at rest, Aulus declared: "It is a common transport, achieved with trivial mediumistic energies. The friend who brought us flowers could do that, and also collect them, using a small amount of ectoplasm that he held between the thumb and index finger of both hands."

"It is important to observe," said Hilario, "how easily ectoplasm goes through dense matter. When our companion used it between his fingers, he had no difficulty crossing the wall."

"Yes," replied the mentor, "ectoplasm is extremely subtle and adheres to our nature, acquiring a dynamic renovated form when used."

"And if the medium were the object of the transport, would he too be able to penetrate the wall in the same conditions?"

"Without a doubt, as long as it is attempted under our control and he is sustained by and associated with our forces. We have, in our sphere, competent technicians who can dematerialize and reconstruct immediately physical elements, since they are conscious of their own responsibility."

And smiling, he added: "You can't forget that the flowers went through the wall of stone with this kind of assistance. If it were useful, the medium, who serves as a base of our work, could be transferred to the outside with the same facility.

"Physical constructions, similarly to those in our sphere, are not entirely solid. Space exists in all forms and elements can penetrate through it. The day will come when science will be able to reintegrate atomic constructions as well as it is learning to disintegrate them nowadays."

The friends present, always interested in awakening their incarnate brothers toward the realities of the Spirit, re-aligned the medium with his carnal body. The young man, still smiling and drowsy, massaged his face. The calming effects of the spiritual passes, however, caused him to fall into a deep hypnotic state again.

The ectoplasm again surged from his nose and ears, revitalized and abundant. Some companions moved through to the adjoining room and we followed. There, on a small electric stove, a large pail of boiling paraffin caught our attention.

A spiritual friend, pleasant in appearance, covered his right hand with the malleable paste that flowed abundantly from the medium and materialized it to perfection. Later, he filled it with the heated liquefied paraffin, leaving an excellente mold as a remembrance to the meeting's participants.

A young lady, who greeted us cordially, also worked the ectoplasm. She molded three flowers and submerged them in the heated paraffin. They were left on the table for the participants of the meeting as a dear remembrance of that evening of tolerance and warmth. Some discarnate friends of the assistants brought ocean shells. Delicate perfumes permeated the room, creating a delightful aroma.

The spiritual workers put the medium through complicated magnetic operations to restore the purity of ectoplasm to his physical body. Realizing this, we had questions for the mentor.

"Do all the people on Earth possess this sort of energy? Is it logical to expect more ample manifestations of it in the future? Must this force be directed or could it organize itself under specific conditions?"

Aulus, leaving the closing phase of the work to the other workers, responded:

"Ectoplasm is situated between dense and perispiritual material, as a product of emanations from the soul passing through the body. It is a resource not only of the human soul, but also of all forms of nature.

"In certain human physiological organizations, it appears in greater proportions and relatively mature to produce phenomena as these we observed here. It is an amorphous element but of great potential and vitality. It can be compared to a protoplasmic mass, extremely sensitive and animated by creative principles that function as conductors of electricity and magnetism. These elements invariably subordinate themselves to the medium's thought and will, or to the discarnates or incarnates that synchronize with the mediumistic mind and act upon it.

"Infinitely plastic, it gives partial or total form to the Spirits and allows them to be visible before humans' eyes or a photographic camera. It offers consistency to the threads, canes and other formations, visible or invisible, in levitation phenomena. It substantiates the images created by the medium's mind, or of the companions who assist him with their thoughts and have affinity with him. We should, therefore, be very careful not to give in to evil intelligences, since being managed by Spirits with undignified passions could lead us to painful disturbances."

Calling attention to the medium who was awakening, he announced: "Our friend polarizes the energies from our plane and gives birth to totally or partially materialized Spirits. They draw critical resources for their manifestations, temporarily becoming his genuine children."

Understanding the concept, Hilario said enthusiastically: "That would lead us to think that the generating forces, exuded by the medium and by the cooperators from our sphere will lead us to fundamental principles of human genetics, in a way that earthly science is not yet aware of."

"Yes, without a doubt," confirmed the mentor, "the principles are the same, although the aspects may be different. The future holds admirable achievements of this nature for us. Let us work and study."

Our disposable time was over. Aulus ended his notable exposition and invited us to leave.

29

Notations About the Service

We returned to Aulus' home. It occurred to me to ask for his opinion regarding the many problems faced by those dedicated to the study of mediumship on Earth.

In the mentor's company we had rapidly received a secure and palpable education. Among incarnates and discarnates, we closely examined many phenomena: the assimilation of mental currents; psychophony or trance communication; possession; out of body experience; clairvoyance; clairaudience; healing forces; telepathy; psychometry, and materialization.

In addition, we were exposed to some themes of tremendous importance to mediumship: the power of prayer; mental fixation; the emergence of the sub-conscious; lycanthropy; obsession; fascination; the law of cause and effect; the out of body experience on the death bed, and the vicious forces.

We studied these without having to resort to complicated terminology. Although we have a deep regard for human science, we questioned why it used confusing terminology for common occurrences, when simpler ones would be clearer.

For example, the metapsychists called occult cryptic sensitivity *cryptestesia*, baptized the knowledge of facts without the aid of the carnal senses with the word *metagnomia*, and divide mediums (*subjects/sujets*, in the terminology of some investigators) into two categories: those with *psychological non-habitual faculties* and those with *mechanical-physical-chemical faculties*. Why not simplify these expressions? Mediumship is, I reflected, in the interest of the entire human race.

Mulling over these thoughts, Aulus received my mental criticism and said:

"Mediumship is undoubtedly our common patrimony; however, each individual and group uniquely register this reality. Spiritism approaches it with Evangelical simplicity based on the clear teachings of Jesus.

"Christ was in constant contact with forces invisible to the common human being during His time on Earth. He cured the obsessed, raised the sick, conversed with the great materialized instructors on the Tabor Mount, listened to the celestial messengers at Gethsemane, and communicated with his disciples after His death on the cross. In spite of this, science still uses experiments to analyze mediumship."

"After a brief pause, he continued: "It does not matter if the learned give different names to what is true. What is important is the sincere desire to be righteous. The laborious effort of science is as sacred as the heroism of faith. Intelligence with the balance and the retort also lives to serve the Lord. By investigating and categorizing mediumistic phenomena, it will be possible to register psychic vibrations, guaranteeing the dignity of religion in the New Era."

I did not, however, want to discuss science, since the end of our study was near. This was the last night that we could enjoy the company of our wise mentor and I wanted to hear only subjects related to mediumship itself. I engaged the mentor in the following dialogue.

I began: "It is fair to say that science does not examine the mediumistic field from our point of view. Logic and experimentation travel on different paths from those of intuition. Nonetheless, even among the followers of Spiritualism, mediumship suffers various interpretations."

"What are you trying to say, Andre?" asked the mentor, affectionately.

"I am recalling those brothers and sisters that refer to mediums as insane. They suggest segregating the students of truth in temples of doctrinaire initiation and place them at a cautious distance from ill and ignorant patients worldwide."

"Ah, yes," said Aulus, "each sanctuary of religious initiation is a venerable place for distribution of spiritual light. Within it those that try to escape from the law of cooperation, however, isolate themselves in an ivory tower of pride that traps them in nets of bright and sterile discussions.

"Such companions are like travelers together on a perilous island, while valiant sailors of goodness perspire and suffer in search of the correct routes toward the continent of fraternity and peace. They rest comfortably under the shade of trees, nurtured with the easy product of the chase and the fresh water they find at hand. They are ecstatic visualizing the greatness of the Universe or uselessly philosophizing.

"But the day will come when a tidal wave will invade their provisional home and take them to the ocean in order to make them re-start."

I continued: "Many studious people from our sphere of work on Earth teach that it should be cultivated only the association with superior souls of the spiritual world. They categorize vulgar mediumistic manifestations as obsession and illness that, in their opinion, do not merit attention."

Aulus said: "This is a convenient attitude that culture encourages. Obsession is a mind disease, but could Medicine cure by forgetting to fulfill its duties? The true superior souls of the spiritual world will never abandon those who suffer and the simple ones. Just as the Sun shines on the palace as well as the hut with the same silent devotion, they aid all in the name of Providence.

I continued: "There are many spiritualist companions that do not tolerate primitive manifestation. If the medium does not go along with their desires, displaying misunderstanding and incompetence, they depart from him in disgust and designate important expressions of spiritual phenomena as fraudulent or void of authenticity. Aulus smiled and added: "They are probably those that avoid hard work. They ignore that the wise individual once had to learn the alphabet, and they curse the child that still cannot read.

"Such friends, Andre, forgot the help they received in grade school. They solicit easy ways, as much as the morphine addict seeks drugs, and become addicted to deplorable attitudes towards life. They look out for themselves and do not respect the obligation to assist those who find themselves in an inferior grade."

I said: "There are those who say that Spiritism is wrong to assist the unbalanced and the ill. They say it gives the impression that by aiding the sick their temples of study and prayer are vast asylums for the mentally ill.

Aulus said: "It is those who desert service to their neighbor that get this wrong impression. Medicine does not lessen because it aids the sick. Being it an honor to the hospitals where it is practiced, it is strengthened by the value of the help it gives to the sick.

"Spiritism cannot be responsible for the many imbalanced people who come to it in search of help. Similarly, we cannot accuse the medical doctor as causing sickness. It is important to recognize that in Spiritism we are the benefactor of tortured mediumship and of the sick minds, providing the balm and the indispensable illumination toward readjustment.

"It is very simple to invent theories to liberate us from our obligation to serve others. It is very difficult, however, to use our mind and hands to carry out the superior principles that we embrace. If our recuperation as well as that of the world were limited to beautiful words, Jesus, who constitutes our daily model, would not have had to come to encounter the needy of the Earth. It would have been enough to send angelical proclamations to the human race without directly experiencing its ignorance and problems.

"Fortunately, conscientious and sensible spiritualists are learning that our goal is to revive the Gospel in its pure and simple form. The Lord does not concede us the treasure of faith so that we can believe and speak, but rather so that we can be prepared to propagate righteousness. To do this, we must begin with ourselves."

I said: "There are also those who affirm that in cases of obsession, the Law of cause and effect intervenes implacably and it is not worthwhile to intervene in favor of a tormented mediumship.

Aulus responded: "That is an argument of well-nurtured selfishness. It would be similar to abandoning the sick because they are debtors under Divine law. We all try to lessen our past debts and we understand that unjustified pain is nonexistent. If only pure love and incessant service can conduct us to redemption, how could those of us marching ahead of our companions in pain abandon them in the name of the principles that also act upon us?

"Today it is the neighbor who suffers the consequences of his past actions; tomorrow, we will be the ones who receive the result of attitudes that dishonored us in the past and that now afflict us. If cooperation is lacking between victims on the difficult road, surely the task of salvation will be longer and more difficult for each of us.

I said: "Some believe that we should not attend to the complex problems of mediumship, since it is said that each should seek the truth himself or herself. They affirm that religions are no more than crutches and that no one has the right to ask the instructors for their assistance regarding his or her personal orientation."

Aulus gestured good humouredly and said: "This would be similar to eliminating schools and reviling the inherent love manifested in creation. Any dignified religion is a sanctuary in which the soul can be educated and conducted through a gradual development toward immortality.

"Let us imagine a big country where parents and teachers did not offer moral and cultural guidance to millions of children, alleging that it is each person's duty to seek virtue and wisdom himself or herself. Let us imagine also a field full of sick people and imminent doctors recommending that they themselves should restore their own health, so leaving them to their individual luck. Where would the logic of such measures be?

"Interdependence is at the base of all of life. The strong is the tutor of the weak. The wise are responsible for the ignorant. Children cannot get along without their parents."

The mentor took a few moments and proceeded: "Not all people possess the identical spiritual age. Terrestrial humanity, as a collective soul, still finds itself far from an angelic state, as far as animal aggressiveness is from human reasoning. It is premature for human beings to appropriate for themselves the right to appeal before absolute truth.

"For now, it is essential that one works with ardent and profound devotion to righteousness, in order to discern the fragmentary and provisional realities of physical life. Therefore, we may be certain that the absence of schools of the spirit, or the suppression of instructors, would multiply the need for hospices and result in a relaxation of the moral level. Without the call for an individual's dignification through mental growth and spiritual purification, we would only stagnate in life's inferior positions."

We were nearing the end of our trip. The mentor's sanctuary home was now in sight.

"Let us work good heartedly," the mentor said, "time conjugated with good service is the foundation of our victory."

The following day Aulus would depart to a place far away, complying with an elevated mission. Because of this, he promised us a farewell embrace on the following morning.

30

The Final Pages

Accompanying our mentor, we now reflected on our imminent separation. Hilario and I were moved and preoccupied. The Sun's first soft rays streamed over the fields on Earth, bathing them in its radiance.

Silent and expectant, we passed a farmer tilling the land with a plough. Aulus pointed to him and broke the silence, murmuring:

"Look! As an instrument of life, mediumship appears everywhere. The farmer is the medium of the harvest, the plant is the medium of the fruit, and the flower is the medium of perfume. We give and receive everywhere, filtering the resources that surround us and modeling them according to our abilities."

We continued and in a few moments, we came to a small carpentry shop. Our mentor pointed out the operator who was modeling an enormous piece of wood, and observed:

"In the craftsman, we have the medium of useful and beautiful things. In his or her devotion to the job, the level of comfort that civilization enjoys today is born."

A little farther on, we saw a small marble factory, where a young man was using a chisel to create a form out of stone.

"There is a sculptor," said Aulus, "the medium of the masterpiece. Art is the mediumship of that which is beautiful, in whose achievements we encounter sublime visions of a future still hidden from us."

The mentor continued making important reflections on the subject, when we passed by some workers in charge of public hygiene. They were removing trash from a great plaza.

"Here we have the street sweepers," he said respectfully, "valiant mediums of cleanliness."

Later, we turned toward a building which functioned as a Court of Justice, and our mentor expressed:

"In the Court of Justice, the judge is the medium of the law. All human beings, in their activities, professions and associations are instruments of forces to which they are dedicated. They produce in accordance with the superior or inferior ideals that inspire them, and attract invisible elements around them according to the sentiments and ideas that nurture them."

We arrived at the home where Hilario and I would dedicate ourselves to helping a sick child. The mentor was expected at some distant place and had to leave us.

Aulus' bearing was fatherly as he followed us to the house. Entering the home, we saw an older gentleman and his wife having breakfast, accompanied by their three small children. Next to a clean and frugal table, a tired and pale child rested in a large chair. He was our patient.

The mentor fixed his eyes on the expressive picture that attracted our attention and exclaimed:

"The blood family is a reunion of souls evolving, readjusting, perfecting or sanctifying. When the man and the woman consider matrimony a school of love and work, and honor the commitments they assume before universal harmony, they are transformed into mediums of life itself. They are responsible for the ongoing materialization of former friends and adversaries, now united, as children and siblings, in the sanctuary of home.

"Dignified paternity and maternity on Earth constitute a priesthood of the highest level for the reincarnated Spirit. Through them, clear and certain regeneration and progress become a reality. Outside the home, it would be difficult to find a place where mediumship is more spontaneous and pure. Man and woman become true creditors of the titles of father and mother when they learn to seek sublimity by giving themselves up for the souls that manifest themselves, through them, as their children on Earth."

And in a beautifully inspired moment, he concluded: "Family can be compared to a reunion for spiritual service in space and time, chiseling hearts for the eternal life."

The mentor then looked at the clock and said: "Those who are responsible must not forget the time."

He left hurriedly and we followed him to the nearby plaza. Aulus observed the Sun's light, as if it were dissolving in a shower of quintessence gold. He was going to embrace us when he perceived my most intimate intention. Then he said, humbly:

"Please, say a prayer for us, Andre."

I, therefore, reverently asked out loud:

"*Dear Jesus:*

Make us worthy of those who spread truth and love.

Increase the treasures of wisdom in the souls who grow in the assistance to their neighbor.

Aid those who give themselves up, distributing hope and peace in Your Name.

Teach us how to honor your faithful disciples with the respect and warmth they deserve.

Crush from the field of our souls, the harmful grass of indiscipline and pride so that humility can favor our renewal.

Do not allow us to confide in our personal blindness, and guide our steps toward those who evolve by humbling themselves and who, because of their nobility and greatness in your presence, do not feel diminished to show themselves as insignificant in their desire to aid us.

Glorify them Father, crowning their heads with your laurels of light."

The mentor must have realized that he personified for us those benefactors whose greatness I had defined, but I hesitated to pronounce his name. Such was the honor that he merited.

When the prayer was over and I looked at him, I was tearful. Aulus did not say a word, and he seemed dressed in a loftier radiance. He bid us goodbye in prayer, held us in one full embrace, and departed. Just as children, Hilario and I, in a mute cry of gratitude, watched him until his figure faded away in the distance.

And then, remembering the task that awaited us and praising our blessed work, we went to assist the sick child, as if we were joined in the great future.

This book was printed
in the Graphical Department of
FEDERAÇÃO ESPÍRITA BRASILEIRA
in the city of Rio de Janeiro,
Brazil, May, 2006.

www.febnet.org.br